The Habits of Trout

The Habits of Trout

AND OTHER UNSOLVED MYSTERIES

Tim Schulz

UPTROUT PRESS
HOUGHTON, MICHIGAN

To Roxanne, Daniel and Matthew:

I hope these stories will help you understand.

Contents

Preface   v

The Last Saturday in April   1

He Was After Walleye   7

The Grass Is Sweeter   12

Back to School   17

It Looked Like He Knew What He Was Doing   22

Everything's Amazing and These Guys Are Happy   28

Marginal Water for Trout   32

Voelker's Nijinsky   38

Sincerity   49

The Good Old Days   53

The Trout Will Let You Know   57

Jerry's Rod   61

Small Stream Sisu   66

Keith   70

Atlantis Found   75

Mañana   79

We Said We Were Going Fishing and We Did   83

How to Catch the Biggest Brook Trout of Your Life   89

It's About Time   93

A Fish Called Dave   97

Growing Older but Not Up   104

The Greenhorn   108

Secrets   112

Fishing with a Worm   117

Trophies   121

How to Catch the Biggest Brook Trout of Your Life, Again   126

The Last Day   130

Preface

TODAY is the last Saturday in April, which, supposedly, is the opening day of Michigan's trout season. But here in the Keweenaw Peninsula—the upper peninsula of Michigan's Upper Peninsula—a foot of snow still blankets my yard, and the Weather Channel says we are under a River Flood Warning. So, instead of fishing for my beloved trout, I'm fishing for a way to tell you, the reader, about this book.

This is a book about fishing. It's a book about fishing for the things in life that are hard to catch, hard to hold, and—ultimately—hard to let go. Trout, I believe, are but one of those things.

When I moved to the Upper Peninsula over 25 years ago, the first books I read about fishing in this region were John Voelker's *Trout Madness* and Jerry Dennis' *A Place on the Water*. Voelker taught me about humility; Dennis taught me about hope. Voelker was a great trout fisherman; Dennis still is. At the core of all great fishermen is an understanding of what can and cannot be understood about things that are precious, and the first words I read in the preface for Voelker's *Trout Madness* explained this succinctly:

There is a lot of amiable fantasy written about trout fishing, but the truth is that few men know much if anything about the habits of trout and little more about the manner of taking them.

When I began fishing for trout, the little I thought I knew about their habits and the manner of taking them was clearly wrong, and, accordingly, I caught very few fish. Over time I learned to catch more fish, and I learned to catch bigger fish, but—like Voelker—I've come to accept that I will never completely understand the habits of trout.

There was a time when I believed I could solve the mysteries of trout in particular and of life in general. But now I think we sometimes need to get skunked. We need to break our line on a good fish every now and again, and sometimes we need to cast all day without a take. We need to be grounded by the humility of failure so we can be lifted by the hope of success.

Every good fisherman I've known has understood how to find humor in the most frustrating circumstances. Jimmy Buffett once said:

Tragedies very often become comedies, and they better become comedies real fast or else you're in a lot of trouble.

Jimmy Buffett, you see, is an excellent fisherman.

Those are the lessons I want to share with you in this book. Along the way I'll tell you about some fish that I've caught and some fish that I've lost. Mostly, though, I'll tell you about the things that only happen when you stop *wish'n you were a fish'n* and just go.

I once had a professor who liked to say, "The way to succeed is to increase your rate of failure." I didn't know it then, but he must have been a trout fisherman.

Tim Schulz
Houghton, Michigan
2018

The Last Saturday in April

THE IDEA OF ROYALTY has never appealed to me, so on the 29th day of April in 2011—when more than two billion people supposedly watched Catherine Middleton marry the Duke of Cambridge—I was among the four billion who sighed a princely "meh." While Kate became The Duchess, I packed and planned for the opening of the Michigan trout season. Six long months of Copper Country winter had dumped enough snow to keep me and most other rod-waving scoundrels from harassing the brook, brown, and rainbow trout that swim in the Upper Peninsula's ponds, lakes and streams. But on the 30th day of April an army of anglers would attack those waters with an arsenal of worms, spinners, streamers, and flies, and I would be there too.

I'd take the usual stuff: rods, reels, flies, waders, nets, and an assortment of "must have" fishing gadgets that I'd either forgotten how to use or never bothered to learn in the first place. But this year I was after something more than trout, so I stocked the truck with topographic maps, plat books, notebooks, cameras, and other tools that would help me document the madness and rediscover the magic that John Voelker—writing under the pen name Robert Traver—chronicled in his books *Trout Madness* and *Trout Magic*. I stumbled upon Voelker's books shortly after I moved to the Upper Peninsula, and my growing obsession with his stories, or "yarns" as he preferred to call them, had finally driven me to action.

John Voelker's professional achievements as a best-selling author and Supreme Court Justice for the State of Michigan, along with his larger-than-life personality and infectious grin, caused Charles Kuralt—a man who made a career out of interviewing great people—to call Voelker "about the nearest thing to a great man I've ever known."

My obsession with Voelker's life and stories is sometimes hard for me to understand, and even harder for others to understand about me, but my friend Jerry Dennis summarized it well when he wrote:

> *That a man of Voelker's intelligence and stature could be so devoted to fishing has been an inspiration to multitudes of the overworked and under-recreated. By his example he gave us permission to have more fun.*

I had a simple plan. I would immerse myself in the roads, bogs, ponds, creeks, and rivers that are scattered throughout the land that Mr. Voelker described as "a forgotten region which was virtually ignored in the westward surge of population." Indeed. If whitetail deer could vote, a referendum to end the deer season in the Upper Peninsula would have passed by a landslide long ago. In this place mostly forgotten by time, I could bounce half naked on a carpet of moss, sing with a choir of spring peepers, and fish for the stories that Voelker and his pals had long ago interred beneath the cold dark waters of some isolated river bend.

On the morning of the First Day, I reluctantly tended to the pomp and circumstance of endowing the world with another hatch of Michigan Tech engineers. This is the sort of thing you'll find on my enjoyment spectrum somewhere between a stubbed pinky toe and rush hour in Los Angeles, but I listened patiently while an old man—who had evidently fashioned a distinguished career out of clichéd proclamations—advised those kids to believe in themselves, never settle, question everything, and dare to live their dream. Upon his declaration that "this is not the end, but the beginning," a muted moan simmered in the audience, then veered into cheerful applause when the crowd realized the man was talking about the graduates' careers, not his speech.

Immediately after that climactic part where the graduates yell and toss their caps into the air, I traded my cap and gown for a waxed-cotton hat and musty fishing vest, pointed my truck toward Marquette County and shouted "giddy-up" as I began my quest to find Camp Alice on Moose Creek, the inspiration for John Voelker's story "Lost Atlantis":

> *Moose Creek is no great shakes to look at, being for the most part narrow and brushy, but the stretch where I usually hit it is a wide shallow stream formed by an ancient inactive beaver dam which backs up water for nearly a mile.*

During one particularly scorching summer day, the story goes, the judge's wife granted a delay on his sentence of two hours hard labor behind a lawn mower, which he took advantage of by commandeering his fish car directly to Camp Alice on Moose Creek. Once there, he paddled a rubber raft upstream toward the headwaters, hoping to find some old beaver dams and new adventures. After slogging through numerous downfalls and tiny dams, Captain Meriwether Lewis of Moose Creek made his discovery. Standing on eight feet of crisscrossed beaver cuttings and "delighted as a kid who had wandered into a fairy toyland," he caught a limit of oversized brook trout with the flawless efficiency of one cast per fish. When the sun's rays began to fade, he pushed upward toward the secluded beginnings of Moose Creek, only to find a family picking blueberries next to a busy road. Moose Creek, he learned, wound about in a gigantic U shape, and his Lost Atlantis was but a stone's throw from the highway.

I couldn't find Moose Creek anywhere within 100 miles of Ishpeming, and most of my inquiries about something called Camp Alice came up empty. Dislike for strangers—especially those who have the slightest appearance of a revenuer—is a thing of legend in the old south, but the backwoods of the Upper Peninsula is still home to many undisclosed distilleries and poaching camps, so selective suspicion is a well-practiced instinct here too. Eventually, though, my persistence paid off and an unusually helpful resident of those woods offered a lead on Camp Alice. "Ah, da Camp Alice? Sure, I know deez one. She not far from da place where Yawny Smit make wood forda weenter. Look here deez map. I show ya."

My new friend was right. Not only did Johnny Smith make wood for the winter near Camp Alice, it appeared that Johnny Smith now owned Camp Alice. Unfortunately, however, he used some of his wood to make signs, and one of those signs hung on a cable inviting everyone including me to keep the hell out of Camp Alice.

I needed a Plan B. According to my plat book a logging company owned the land on the opposite side of Moose Creek, and another map revealed a seasonal road ending within a mile of the creek. The road wasn't gated, but the opening of trout season is typically a week or two before the opening of seasonal roads, and this was, alas, a typical year. Oh well. I planned to return in a few weeks with John Voelker's grandson Adam Tsaloff, and the road would be open by then.

I retreated to Ishpeming for dinner at Congress Pizza, a restaurant and bar founded by John Voelker's dear friend Louis Bonetti, the gullible guide in Voelker's story "The Voyage". Louis' grandson Paul tended the bar and gladly shared stories and old photographs of his grandfather and the judge. By the time I stopped eating pizza, drinking beer, and gawking at those old pictures I was too tired to search the back roads for a makeshift campsite, so I drove to Marquette and parked my truck in the Walmart parking lot. Nestled between an eighteen-wheeler and a horse trailer, I wasn't exactly *out there* but the bourbon from my old tin cup did taste better.

About two hours after I fell asleep, I awoke to the sound and lights of another car settling into in an adjacent spot. I raised my head slightly and strained my eyes, but without my glasses my new neighbors looked like four long-necked aliens with small elongated heads sitting in the space between the two front seats. With my glasses, I saw that the four long necks were legs, and the bodies attached to those legs were in the back seat where two normal-sized heads were locked in a passionate pre-mating kiss.

This, I should have known, is the way adventures work. Sure, you can plan and scheme and try to make things turn out the way you want them to, but the best adventures often unfold at times and in places that you don't expect. You carefully plan and conspire to court the girl of your dreams, then painfully learn that that dream is a nightmare. But when you reluctantly agree to meet your roommate's girlfriend's college friend—even though you're afraid that "she's pretty and nice too" probably means she is neither—you fall in love and spend the rest of your life with that girl. Sometimes you just need to show up.

I awoke at 6 a.m. to the sound of some kid pushing around an electric machine that gathered up shopping carts while my camp-mate rolled his eighteen-wheeler slowly toward highway 41. My naughty neighbors' show had long since ended, so I jumped in the front seat of my truck and drove to McDonald's to eat breakfast and take a pee. After that I'd paddle upstream and search for my own lost paradise, and I'd try to not miss the ones that are hiding in plain sight.

He Was After Walleye

CATCH AND RELEASE is difficult to explain to someone who has never gone fishing with a deliberate plan to release everything they catch. Opposable thumbs and a three-pound brain have enabled us to invent spectacular and efficient ways to feed ourselves, and some people can't understand why other people use those methods to play with their food.

I've fished for as long as I can remember, and during my formative years I never released a fish. I sometimes threw the small ones back—in the most literal sense of the expression—but I never released them. I learned to fish from my mom, and because she grew up poor during the Great Depression, a lake for her was what a grocery store was for someone with money.

One of my regrets as a father is that I haven't fished more with my kids. This, I tell myself, is because the bugs usually bite more than the fish, because the gratification is rarely immediate, or because fishing is simply boring for them, but I know it is possible, and maybe even likely, that I just haven't tried enough. Like most people do, I make too many excuses about things that are more in my control than I'd like to believe. Like Thomas Edison is said to have said, we sometimes miss opportunity because it shows up at our door dressed in overalls looking an awful lot like work. I surely missed some of those overall-clad opportunities with my sons, but not all of them.

When the boys were small I'd sometimes paddle them around their grandpa's lake, and if the crappie or bluegill bite was on, they'd catch fish. Sometimes a lot of fish. If the bite wasn't on, which happened often, they'd get bored and I'd let them paddle around in circles until they got tired, then I'd take them back to shore.

Occasionally I'd get the idea that they might like to fish the way I fished, so I'd invite them to some out-of-the-way spot. I once took my youngest son, Matthew, to a place that held a seemingly endless supply of crappie, and he caught a fish on nearly every cast. With a focus and resolve for feeding his family that would have made my mom proud, he filled a bucket with enough fish to feed the two of us, as well as his mother and his brother, and then we walked the mile or so back to the car. Maybe a mile each way was too far to hike for someone with short legs, or maybe the mosquitoes bit him more than they bit me, or maybe a seemingly endless supply of crappie sometimes ends, but, for whatever reasons, we never went back.

We didn't release any fish that day, mostly because the idea of releasing a fish that didn't need to be thrown back was still outside my comfort zone. At some point, though, I noticed that many of the fly fishermen I admired did something incredible when they caught a wonderful fish. They didn't put it on a stringer or chain, they didn't toss it in a cooler, they didn't smack it over the head and put it in a creel. Instead, they handled it gently—or not at all—and let it swim back to where it came from. Simply put, they let it go for the sake of letting it go.

I remember the first time I tried that. One evening, while casting poppers on my wife's family lake, I caught a trophy-sized large-mouth bass. Just like my heroes, I gently removed the popper from the great fish's jaw, admired its color and size, and imagined the fish swimming back into the darkness to patrol its section of lily pads, chasing away pike and eating every bluegill that was stupid enough to drift into its territory. Then I took it back to the farmhouse and we ate it for dinner. The boys said it was delicious.

Eventually, though, I found peace with the idea of releasing a fish that I could otherwise take home to show off and eat. Now I release nearly every fish I catch, but I don't resent anyone who chooses to keep and kill their fish. I'd prefer they left the fish in the river for me to catch, and I certainly won't show them my secret places, but, if it's legal for them to keep the fish they catch, then the decision is theirs. And that's the lesson I've tried to teach my children.

One day in early summer when the kids were still small, I heard that the walleye were biting on Portage Lake and talked the boys into an afternoon outing in our boat. I bought some nightcrawlers and we motored to what I believed were the most likely spots to find walleye. But the action was slow, so I replaced their nightcrawler rigs with Mr. Twisters and we sped off to a place I knew would hold some smallmouth bass. Once I had them casting and retrieving over a rocky drop-off, I made a cast with my fly rod. The popper landed, the ripples settled, I gave it a twitch, and a smallmouth levitated from the bottom and engulfed my fly. The kids hollered and hooted every time the fish jumped, and when I landed it my oldest son, Daniel, lifted the lid to the live well and said "throw it in here."

"I'm going to let this one go," I said.

"Why?" Daniel asked. "I want to eat that one."

"Here's the deal, guys. When someone catches a fish, they get to decide what to do with that fish. If it's a legal fish and they want to

9

keep it, then they can keep it. That's their choice, not yours. Same thing if they want to release it. It's their call."

"But why don't you want to keep it?" Daniel asked.

"Because I always let the smallmouth bass go. When I want to eat a fish, I go after the walleye."

The boys cast a little more, but neither was able to bring up another smallmouth, so I turned on the electric motor and told them to let out some line and we'd troll along the drop-off and see if we could get something that way. About the time they had both lost interest, the line peeled off of Matthew's reel and his rod bent deeply from a snag or something.

The something was a pike that, at times, threatened to pull the little boy's slight frame over the side of the boat. I had adjusted his drag to a light setting, so it took him a long time to get the fish close. When he did, I netted the pike and removed the hook, and then Matthew said that he wanted to hold the fish. When his hands had a firm grip on the fish, his brother opened the live well and said "throw it in here." Ignoring Daniel's request, Matthew walked away from the live well to the side of the boat, where he lowered the fish as close to the water as he could and let it go.

"Matt, why did you let that fish go?" his brother asked.

"I don't want a pike," he said. "I'm after walleye."

The Grass Is Sweeter

I love my bamboo fly rod and
I choose to think it has a sneaking yen for me.
John Voelker

THIS IS HOW IT STARTED: "If you have the okay to pull the trigger, I would do it and enjoy the rod for the rest of your life. You could get run over by a moose tomorrow and then where would you be?"

You get advice like that from John Voelker's grandson and you start to think. Only five-hundred moose inhabit the Upper Peninsula, but over four-hundred of them live nearby in Marquette, Baraga, and Iron counties. An adult moose at full speed, I've been told, can have the same momentum as a Prius at 20 miles per hour. I was convinced, but I still needed to secure the "okay to pull the trigger."

"You know, honey," I began. "Adam Tsaloff said I should buy a bamboo fly rod because, if I don't, I could get run over by a moose tomorrow. What do you think about those two options?"

"Do I get to choose?" she replied.

The next day I noticed that her computer's web browser displayed a page for *Code Blue Urge Moose Attractant*, but, as far as I could tell, all of my fishing gear still had the musty smell of neglect rather than the musky smell of moose. Two days later I was still alive and none of my gear was dowsed in that "powerful attractant that will last, won't wash away in the rain, and will keep the moose coming back for more." This, I believed, was an implicit okay to pull the trigger.

On Adam's suggestion, I called Sweetgrass Rods in Montana and asked to speak with Dave Delisi. "Hello Dave. I'm the Tim that Adam told you about and I want a bamboo fly rod please."

"Yes, of course. Let me ask a few questions and we'll find a rod that is perfect for you," Dave replied. This was definitely much better than being run over by a moose.

Sweetgrass was the perfect place to buy my first bamboo fly rod. For more than thirty years, Glenn Brackett hand-crafted bamboo fly rods for the R.L. Winston Rod Company, but, in 2006, Glenn and Jerry Kustich left Winston to start Sweetgrass. Demand for the Boo Boys' "artisanal craftsmanship" is intense—the waiting time for a custom Sweetgrass rod can be over a year. But, if the stars are aligned just right, you can call them and get one of their Mantra rods delivered in a week or two, and on this day, the stars were aligned.

The rod we agreed on was a 7′9″ hexagonal rod built to cast a 4 or 5 weight line. Adam had suggested that the rod was perfect for me, and, after confirming this with Dave, I signed the papers and began the adoption process. As I anxiously awaited the rod's arrival, Adam—in the dual role of fisherman friend and delivery nurse—outlined his tips for bringing the baby home.

"Hands together to put together. Hands apart to take apart. No twisting at any time. Wipe the rod off when you get home and leave it out to dry in a safe place overnight, then wipe it down again in the morning and put away. Don't mess with the ferrules with anything if you don't need to.

"On the stream treat the rod like a fishing rod, not a vile of nitro. It is at least as strong as any rod you have ever used. The only place bamboo gets broken is between the tube and the stream.

"Remember, however, there is no going back! Once you pull the trigger, you will fish bamboo the rest of your life. You will think, eat, sleep and poop bamboo." Bamboo is part of Adam's bloodline. He inherited many of his grandfather's skills and tendencies: an innate instinct for the roll cast; a fanatical obsession with bamboo fly rods; a magnetic attraction to the locations where wild trout reside; and a wry sense of humor that has a way of uncovering the magic that often gets veiled by the madness. His grandfather once wrote that "to my mind there is no fairy wand in creation more graceful and beautiful than a good bamboo fly rod," and Adam wholeheartedly agrees.

For me, though, bamboo was something new. I grew up fishing cheap fiberglass rods attached to even cheaper Zebco reels. And though I had fly-fished for roughly half my life, all of my rods were made from graphite. The southern Illinois redneck in me—whom I am proud to acknowledge—sorta liked the idea that the advertisements for one of my fly rods said it "shot line like a cannon," and the guy that sold it to me said that I could "really rip some lips with that one." Finer things like wicker creels and handmade rods with wondrously slow action were not part of my heritage. My foray into bamboo was an experiment in nature versus nurture.

"Tim, we have a rod that is all finished except for the reel seat. I can get to that early next week and have the rod out to you before the week is complete." When I read Dave's note it hit me. Dave wasn't telling me that some warehouse in Topeka was about to ship some vacuum-sealed package that contained some rod with a model number that matched the one I had ordered with an 800 number I could call if I had any problems. Dave was telling me that my rod—the one Glenn and Jerry had designed, the one that he, Dana, Wade and Jason had helped build—was about to have a reel seat attached and be mailed to my home.

On the day my new rod arrived, I strung it up and rushed out to practice my cast on the lawn. Just then, Roxanne drove down the driveway and lovingly asked, "Why don't you take your new rod to Van Riper State Park today, honey, or somewhere else near Michigamme? You know, where we saw that moose last month." Oddly, my waders smelled a little musky, so, rather than fish in the center of moose country, I took the Mantra to a local brook trout stream.

As I zigzagged through the woods and down to the river, I worried that a rogue branch would reach out and snap off my new rod's tip in some kind of wood-versus-wood tribal assault. "Worthy of Trust and Confidence" is the motto for the Secret Service, and I was prepared to take a stick in the eye or whatever was necessary in the service of protecting my new rod. Adam said the only place bamboo gets broken is between the tube and the stream, so I guarded the rod with my life. Safely on the stream, I began to cast.

"Each rod has its own personality and will communicate how it prefers to be cast, if you listen," Dave had instructed. And just as he warned, the rod stubbornly refused to respond to the ungraceful sequence of double hauls that I regularly used to propel line with my other rods. The rod insisted that I let it do the work, and, when I complied, its response was immediate. The compact loop of line unrolled perfectly above the tiny creek, avoiding the ego-killing grasp of the tag alders as though it had a mind that could recognize and avoid those obstacles, then it placed the tiny caddis right where I hoped it would land. A brook trout expressed its approval with a splashy assault, and when I removed the hook from the fish's mouth and released it in a few inches of water, it rubbed its head against the rod like a cat purring its approval. The rod was everything I hoped it would be and everything I now believed a rod should be. Adam was right. I would fish bamboo the rest of my life.

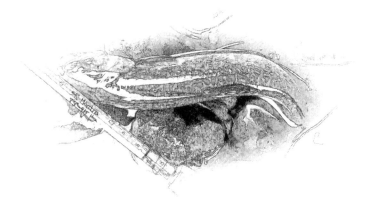

Back to School

IT STARTS IN AUGUST. The mighty yellow Blue Bird and Thomas Built buses rise from a three-month hibernation to begin their daily shuttle routines. Just a few at first, but then more and more until September ends and the metamorphosis is complete. The nation is back in school.

I should be used to this by now. I was a student for more than twenty years and have been a teacher for twenty more. But participating in the autumn ritual as a pupil or professor is substantially different from presiding over it as a parent. You begin by filling their backpacks with pencils, paper, Pokey-somebody cards, and all the other items those all-grown-up-now children say they need. They hop on the bus and you smile.

I am young; life is long; the autumn of my year is exciting.

Then—with little or no warning—you check and recheck the oil, the tires, and every other part of the late model used car that you've commissioned to take your oldest child on a ten-hour trip to a new kind of school and a different kind of life. They hop in the car and you frown.

17

I am old; life is short; the autumn of my existence is frightening.

And so it was that Roxanne and I were set to escort Daniel on his return to Michigan State University, when, one morning in late July, my email inbox contained an inconvenient invitation:

```
We will hold a workshop with key academic and
administrative personnel on Friday, August 26.
Your attendance is required.
```

Suddenly we had no choice. The sophomore Spartan would drive south with his mother on Thursday; I would remain in Houghton to prepare for Friday's bothersome obligation.

On the evening that my wife and son departed for East Lansing, my youngest son Matthew was away practicing with his band, so I—overwhelmed by solitude and loneliness—retreated to my office to wallow in sadness and self-pity.

"Stop whining you big sissy. Let's go fishing."

The challenge came from the southeast corner of my office, but the only thing there—animate or inanimate—was a rack of fly rods. I had never won an argument with a fly rod, and this was not going to be my first. Fishing new water and spending several hours in the car was the perfect prescription for my condition, so the cheeky rod and I headed off toward a distant river that I'd always wanted to fish. If the rod kept quiet, I just might think my way through the sadness.

The drive to the river would take more than two hours, but if I didn't dawdle and dally I would have an hour or two to fish. Here at the 47th parallel in Michigan's Upper Peninsula, we see nearly sixteen hours of daylight each day from late May through mid July. But now—in late August—the sun lingers for only thirteen hours and discards three minutes a day from the length of its stay. The endless summer begins to wane.

As I drove I thought about my sons. Neither Daniel nor Matthew is a fly fisherman. Both have fished, and at times they've done so with enthusiasm, but fishing in general has been a small part of their lives, and fly fishing in particular has played no role. Until earlier this year, that is, when Daniel returned from college in May and asked if he could join me for a few days during my spring camping trip on the Escanaba River, and I happily agreed.

Strong winds and few rising fish set the stage for disappointment on our first evening. But just before dark the winds subsided, his casting improved, and a couple fish rose within range. He cast to one and it took.

Fish on . . . tight line . . . ping . . . fish off.

"That's okay, son. Until you do this a few times you can't know how to fight a fish on a fly rod. I told you this would likely happen." He flashed an uncomfortable smile as I tied on a new fly, and his hands shook slightly as he took the fly and began to search for another fish. We spotted one within range and he cast.

Fish on . . . too much slack . . . fish off.

"That's okay, son. That's how it usually goes. The first fish breaks off. The second fish gets off because you give it too much slack. Now you are ready to land one." He smiled more uncomfortably and his hands shook less slightly as he cast yet again.

Fish on . . . fish in.

I relived that night two or three times during the long drive to the river. I knew Daniel's and Matthew's lives would get busier and fuller with each new year, and our fishing trips would be few and far between. But after the final exams and before the summer internships, perhaps we'd wade side-by-side again.

I made it to the river around eight p.m. Far more bugs were dancing in the air and on the water than I had expected, and, more important, several trout were steadily sucking those bugs from the surface. Some of the fish were large, and, because I was using my new bamboo rod that I'd only tested on a small local stream, I was thrilled by the prospect of hooking and fighting a forceful fish with this rod. Six fish on. Six fish in. That night the bamboo gods were kind.

Roxanne wouldn't return from East Lansing until Saturday, and Matthew was planning to spend the weekend with friends, so when I was paroled from Friday's momentous meeting, I fueled the truck and made the long drive back to the river. Although I had landed every fish I hooked the night before, some had ignored my offerings, and one of those was large.

Fewer bugs were in the air and on the water when I returned, but the largest fish was rising again. On the previous evening all the trout I caught had taken a small caddis, but this brute had shown no interest in that fly. Now I spotted a small dark mayfly on the water, extended my 5x tippet with a foot or two of 6x and tied on a size 18 parachute Adams.

Slurp!

I knew immediately that the fish was huge, but I was stunned when it jumped. Well over 20 inches in length; probably over 25; maybe close to 30. It had likely eaten trout that were larger than any I had ever hooked on a dry fly. Its shoulders were stout, and when it erupted from the water it looked more like a steelhead than a brown trout.

Ping.

The sound rang out while the fish was still in the air. I stood motionless and felt ill as I watched my fly-less line float downstream. Dejected, I decided to reel in and head home, but another fish rose about ten feet below where the giant had been feeding. I tied on another small Adams and cast.

Fish on . . . too much slack . . . fish off.

"That's okay, son. This is how it usually happens. The first fish breaks off. The second fish gets off because you give it too much slack. Now you're ready to land one."

I, too, was back in school.

It Looked Like He Knew
What He Was Doing

I HAVE A FRIEND who casts a fly for neither distance nor accuracy nor stealth. Aside from those limitations he's a splendid fisherman. It's not for lack of strength or dexterity or intellect that he fly-casts with less than average skill. Warren is a farm boy from Catawba, Wisconsin, and he has the farm-boy frame you'd expect: bone, muscle and gristle. In his forties he learned to play ice hockey and fly airplanes. He has a PhD in physics, teaches at Michigan Tech, and travels the world lecturing about a subject he calls "energetic materials," something you or I would call "explosives" or "bombs." Warren shouldn't be such a crappy fisherman. He just doesn't fish enough.

When he's not in Pullman or Boston or Basel or Turino, Warren usually joins me in early summer for a camping trip on the Escanaba River. We fish, drink scotch, tell stories, play cribbage, and sleep, usually, but not always, in that order. One morning during a recent trip—before we started fishing or drinking or telling or playing—Warren learned that a tree had fallen on a friend's shed. Warren generally jumps at the chance to help a friend in need; he hops and skips when it requires him to use his tractor.

"I need to run into town for a few hours. I should be back in time for the evening hatch. Don't wait for me if I'm late. I'll catch up with you on the river."

"Do you have enough flies?" I asked.

"Sure."

He proudly flashed a small plastic box that held one black Woolly Bugger, two Zug Bugs, two Prince nymphs, a worn-out Muddler Minnow, and three large Royal Wulffs. "If those don't work, I have plenty of Scotch." He patted my back, winked, and leapt into his car. A toxic cloud of cigar smoke billowed through the window of the battered old Omni, and then he was gone.

By the time Warren returned from his trip to town, I was waist-deep in the Escanaba River, straining to solve a demoralizing hatch. Steady winds and intermittent rains kept all but the tiniest bugs off the water; only teeny flies, wispy tippets, and perfect drifts could catch a fish on this un-enchanted evening. The fishing was tough and technical, and I worked hard to hook a small fish every half hour or so. What the heck would Warren do? The smallest fly in his box was a size 14 Royal Wulff, and his tippet diameter was determined by the number of times he cut off and retied a fly to his lone tapered leader. He was screwed.

Not that a better fly inventory would matter. Warren loves the Royal Wulff. He loves to fish it in all the wrong ways, in all the wrong places, at all the wrong times. If another aviating angler hadn't invented that fly, Warren would probably fish with spinners or spoons or pork chops.

Like Warren, Lee Wulff was an avid and accomplished pilot. Unlike Warren, Lee Wulff was a fly-fishing innovator. He conceived the fishing vest, popularized left-handed reels, persuaded fishermen that "game fish are too valuable to be caught only once," and developed a prominent style of fly that inherited his name. His most famous pattern—the Royal Wulff—is a colorful and bushy fly that Lee himself described as strawberry shortcake for trout. This is Warren's favorite fly.

Lee's talents and skills—like Warren's—extended far beyond fly fishing. His restless pursuit of education introduced him to engineering at Stanford and art in Paris. He began his career with a New York City advertising agency, but ultimately found fame as an artist and fly-fishing icon.

The fly-fishing community was shocked in 1991 when Lee's single-engine Piper Cub crashed near Hancock, New York. His copilot survived the accident and insisted that the crash had not caused Lee's death; instead, it was Lee's untimely death from a heart attack that had caused the crash.

Thinking about Lee's unfortunate crash reminded me of the time that Warren— who lives near Hancock, Michigan—dodged death while flying a Piper Arrow somewhere between Spokane and Pullman. He was perfecting the maneuvers he would need to demonstrate during an upcoming commercial license exam, and his main objective was to polish a procedure for recovering from a stall.

Cruising at about 4,000 feet above the Palouse prairie, Warren deliberately pulled the Piper's nose upward until the wings stopped carrying the plane. The plane stalled, and, because the clockwise rotation of the engine's propeller pushed more wind under the right wing than the left, the right rose and the left dipped. As the plane commenced its predictable leftward cant, Warren did precisely what he had been taught to do, and exactly what he had done dozens of times before. But something was wrong. The left wing continued to fall until the aircraft entered a life-threatening spin.

Although recovering from a spin is too dangerous to practice, Warren had read enough to know what to do. He pushed the buttons and switches he needed to push. He pulled the levers and knobs he needed to pull. He did everything he had read about that would stop the plane from spinning, and his calm and resourceful actions caused the plane to cease spinning and resume flying. Unfortunately, however, the Piper was on a vertical flight path and pointed straight for the prairie floor. Without panic, Warren forcefully raised the plane's nose and the aircraft leveled with 1500 feet to spare. The entire ordeal lasted less than 15 seconds.

My remembrance of Warren's heroics reminded me that he was a brave and capable pilot. But it also reminded me that—despite his mastery of aviation, tractors, and energetic materials—he was not a proficient piscator. He and his nine flies would be no match for this hatch, so I succumbed to the shame, reeled in, and set out in pursuit of my friend. The rain had subsided, but the wind was still strong and the skies were darkening. If I was going to help him catch a fish, I'd have to find him soon. I roamed the river until it was too dark to see, and then reluctantly returned to camp to find Warren relaxing beside a roaring campfire with a cribbage board stationed on a small table between his chair and mine. I was gut-punched by guilt. At least he had some Scotch.

"Hi, Warren. Did you get back in time to do some fishing?"

"Sure." he said.

"How'd you do?" I asked, and readied myself for remorse.

"Great. I caught one fish that was over eighteen inches, one that was about seventeen inches, and several that ranged from twelve to sixteen."

"Really?" I expect a little embellishment in fish camp, but this was ridiculous. I inspected the Scotch bottle. It was nearly full.

"Take a look. I have some photos on my computer."

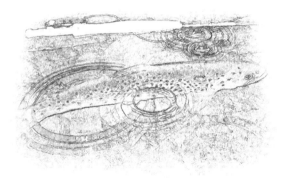

Warren went on to explain that I was busy landing a small trout when he arrived at the river. Not wanting to bother me, he hiked upstream and began fishing above an old log that was a fixture in the river. The wind was gusting in the downstream direction, so Warren attached a big bushy Royal Wulff to his stumpy tippet and let the gale do most of the work. He flipped the colorful fly off to the side of the log and let it skate into the slack water just above the diminutive dam. Nothing happened until it began to rain. But the moment the water's surface was covered with raindrop dimples, hefty trout emerged from the deep water beside the log and assaulted the Royal Wulff on every cast. Warren had returned to camp when he was down to his last Wulff and it looked like the rain had stopped for the night.

"How the heck did you figure that out?" I asked.

"Well, it's sorta like the time I got in that pickle while flying out in Washington. I had never actually done it before, but I remembered reading about it somewhere. So I tied on a Royal Wulff and gave it a try. Holy man, did it work. I'll tell you what, Tim, if someone watched me recover from that spin in Spokane or catch those trout tonight, they'd have to say that it looked like I knew what I was doing."

I sat dumbfounded while Warren stashed his computer in the Omni.

"How'd you do?" he asked. "I bet you cleaned up, too."

"Pass the scotch, friend. Low card deals."

Everything's Amazing and These Guys Are Happy

Everything is amazing right now and nobody's happy.
Louis C.K.

THE MODERN MARVEL OF FLIGHT transports us from New York to San Francisco in under six hours, but—as Louis C.K. observed in his brilliant comedic rant—a twenty-minute delay on the airport apron is an occurrence we remember for its extraordinary cruelty. Humankind's spectacular escape from the Malthusian trap has been undeniably amazing, but many of us remain unhappy. We look every gift horse in the mouth, and, alas, detect at least one long tooth.

Fly fishing—an activity I rate among the most pleasurable of pleasant chores—has not escaped the unappreciative complaints of the golden-haired children among us. Some of us fish for, but rarely catch, that perfect bowl of porridge. The hatches are too sparse or too dense; the weather too hot or too cold; the current too swift or too slow. We convince ourselves that another river, another bend, another fly, or another day must surely be better than this.

For some of us, though, every bowl of porridge is just right for the simple reason that it is, after all, a bowl of porridge. When the weather is cold, we're thankful it's not hot. When it's hot, we're thankful it's not windy. And when it's windy, we're just thankful to be fishing. My friends Dave McMillan and his sons David and Brian are exemplars of this philosophy. When they go fishing, everything's amazing and these guys are happy.

I met Dave for the first time on the river. After casual introductions, one of us went upstream, the other went downstream, and the whole encounter took about two minutes, just the way it should when two fishermen meet on the river. I met Dave for the second time at my campsite. After formal introductions, we sat around the campfire planting the seeds for a new and lasting friendship, and the whole thing took about four hours, just the way it should when two fishermen meet off the river. Since then we've fished and camped together nearly every year. We don't plan and scheme to make sure that our trips are "epic," but they tend to come out just fine.

Mark Twain said that it took him more than three weeks to prepare a good impromptu speech, and Twain's approach to planned spontaneity is common within today's fly-fishing culture. The carefree lifestyle of the modern trout bum is often documented with the aid of camera cranes, zero gravity stabilizers, collapsible reflector discs, and a seemingly endless arsenal of high-tech accessories that capture the slow-motion splendor of every cast, every catch, and every release. Magnificent scenery, introspective commentary, and haunting soundtracks conspire to raise tiny bumps on the arms and legs of all but the most callused and unromantic of souls.

The fishing lives of anglers like Dave and his boys, though, are rarely viewed in high definition with a soothing score of progressive folk guitar. Beyond the bamboo rods and well-stocked fly boxes, their equipment is unsophisticated and spartan. A few cans of beer, a crumpled box of cheap cigars, a tiny bottle of 100 percent DEET, and a couple flashlights with batteries that may or may not be charged. Like W.C. Fields, they also carry a flagon of whiskey to drink in case of snakebite, and—leaving nothing to chance—they bring a small snake.

In their world of unplanned amazement, though, some things are more amazing than others, and an invitation to visit John Voelker's beloved Frenchman's Pond was one of those things, even though—or especially because—an impending thunderstorm rumbled and flashed to the west.

"I always thought I had a better chance of getting struck by lightning than making it to Frenchman's, so you better not stand too close," Dave said while he and his sons stood on the old wooden platforms and cast tiny flies to Frenchman's trout. They stood on platforms because the vegetation around the pond makes it nearly impossible to approach in any other way, and anyone crazy enough to wade the pond would surely disappear into its bottomless muck leaving a soggy hat as the only evidence that they had ever been there. The pond isn't pretty, but it is easy to love. Voelker himself described it this way:

> It isn't very deep, but I love it; the trout aren't very big or many, but I love it; it's scummy and weedy and isn't very pretty, but still I love it.

One by one, Dave and his sons each hooked and landed a trout, crowing with delight each time one of those speckled belles bored for the dark bottom of the fabled pond. When they landed and released the last trout, they kissed the ground and toasted their good fortune with swigs of bourbon from an old tin flask.

After a few photos at the cabin, Voelker's grandson Adam and his good friend James accompanied us to the Escanaba River where, promptly upon our arrival, the deluge caught us. James and I weathered the outburst and managed to catch a couple trout, but Dave and his sons retreated for shelter with Adam where they talked about fishing in general and Adam's grandfather in particular. Sometime during the conversation, Adam said that he was happy they had a chance to visit the pond, and that the McMillan clan were exactly the kind of people that his grandfather would have wanted to fish with.

"Are those guys always so happy to be fishing?" James asked me as we approached the group.

"Only on days that end with a 'y'."

Marginal Water for Trout

WHERE CAN I CATCH A BIG TROUT? I sometimes field this query from fishing friends who seemingly mistake me for a person who is smart enough to know and dumb enough to tell. Our subsequent dialogue generally transpires like a scene from *All the President's Men*:

"Follow the money."

"What do you mean? Where?"

"Oh, I can't tell you that."

"But you could tell me that."

"No, I have to do this my way. You tell me what you know, and I'll confirm. I'll keep you in the right direction if I can, but that's all. Just . . . follow the money."

Whereas Deep Throat instructed Bob Woodward to follow the *money*, I direct my angling investigators to follow the *oxygen*. Trout, you see, consume oxygen like politicians devour money. Find one and you will surely find the other.

From an angler's perspective, the oxygen content of water is determined by two factors: temperature and turbulence. The temperature dependence is governed by something called *Henry's Law*. In simplified terms, the amount of oxygen in water decreases as the temperature increases. Freezing water at the standard sea-level barometric pressure contains about 14 milligrams of oxygen per liter. At 60°F the oxygen concentration falls to about 10 milligrams per liter, and at 70°F it's down to about 9 milligrams per liter. These concentrations are typical of calm, stationary water, though, and for the same reason that swirling a spoon in your coffee causes your java to absorb more sugar, the turbulent water around waterfalls and riffles generally contains more oxygen than the stagnant and slow moving parts of a river or stream. Find a river with cool, fast moving water and you will find more oxygen. Find more oxygen and you will find more trout.

All other things being equal, trout require more oxygen and, hence, cooler water than more heat-tolerant species like smallmouth bass and northern pike. When Earth's mid-summer tilt inevitably provokes the water temperatures to rise above 70°F, the abundance of these more resilient fish helps maintain sanity and preserve domestic tranquility for a trout fisherman stricken with the acute despair that is induced by an uninvited expansion of mercury.

As it always seems to do, the high summer heat had scorched the Upper Peninsula's rivers and streams for several weeks straight when I decided to venture southward to while away a day casting for bass and pike. Most of the nearby rivers and streams flow into Lake Superior, but the southern part of this slender peninsula is drained by a bounty of lovely Lake Michigan tributaries. Many of those, though marginal for trout during the hottest summer months, provide excellent fishing for bass, pike, and other fish that John Voelker uncharitably classified as members of the lobster family. It was on one of those rivers, while attempting to entice a few feisty bass to assault a four-inch-long counterfeit sculpin, that I learned that when it comes to a trout's propensity to avoid warmer water, all other things are not always equal.

My streamer inventory was sadly depleted, so the previous night I had tied three Madonnas—a simple fly with a pearl-flash under-body, a rabbit-strip over-body, and a deer-hair collar and head. I had a few other scraggly streamers that I could use in a pinch, but I hoped that these three would get me through the day.

My preferred method for fishing streamers is to use a sinking line and the jerk-strip retrieve that Bob Linsenman and Kelly Galloup pioneered in their book *Modern Streamers for Trophy Trout*. Jerry Dennis proclaims in the book's forward:

> "It might not make you give up dry flies and floating lines, but as sure as the day is long it will make your previously unproductive hours more productive."

I could not agree more.

The first two bass that attacked the Madonna missed. Part of the fun of Linsenman's and Galloup's method is that, when done properly, you can usually see the streamer—and any accompanying assault—throughout the retrieve. It is visual sport. The first hook-up, though, came when the streamer was out of sight, and the short-lived battle that followed reduced my streamer squadron to two. The line was cut crisply, so I suspected I had been cleaned out by a pike. Two more pike and my Madonna inventory would be exhausted.

The first fish I landed was a chunky smallmouth that devoured the fly just as it hit the water, before I had begun to jerk or strip. Ten minutes later I was onto another, and my ear-to-ear grin divulged a *no matter what happens next this outing will be a success* attitude that now controlled my consciousness. The next fish broke off, but this time the end of my line was branded with the tell-tail curl of a defective knot. I attached my last Madonna, double-checked the knot, then checked the knot again.

I waded downstream toward a fishy looking run, launched the yellow Madonna across the river and began to jerk and strip. A massive torpedo slashed at the fly and missed just as I initiated one of the jerks, leaving me briefly paralyzed by the surprise of the assault. When I moved the streamer again the fish responded with another savage strike. Again, no hookup, but this behavior—coupled with my estimate that the fish was well over two feet long—convinced me that the antagonizer was a pike.

Because pike often assail a fly on successive casts, I had to make a decision. I could lose my last Madonna to this pike, or I could move down-stream and past the toothy brute's lair. What the heck? Pike can be great fun to hook and fight, so I threw caution to the wind and flung my fly along with it.

The attack was spectacular and ferocious. The ensuing explosion sent a shrapnel of water, slime, and scales across the river's surface, and all of my senses signaled that I had hooked a two- to three-foot pike. For an instant I was certain I could smell that musty stench I've come to associate with pike. After our fleeting but tumultuous introduction, the fish bolted toward Lake Michigan.

I was unreasonably calm at this point, mostly in preparation for the inescapable moment when a sharp fang would liberate my last Madonna from my line. Something about this pike, though, was odd. Its head shakes were heavier, and its pulls were longer than those of other pike I'd fought of its size. After a little reeling and a lot of wading, I gradually closed the distance to the fish and was close enough to see the beast's back when it slowly broached the surface. The sight of a brown trout's telltale freckles provoked a sudden strike of incontinence.

My first attempt to land the fish was an embarrassing display of unprepared ineptitude. The widest opening of my landing net was 15 inches, and—with my ability to execute simple arithmetic temporarily suspended—I foolishly used the net to scoop a fish that was roughly twice its length. The result was exactly what a more reasonable person would have foretold—both times I tried. A butterfly net would have worked as well.

I dropped my overmatched net, shifted the rod back to my right hand, then awkwardly crammed my left hand into a mesh fish-handling glove. The fish was still close, but—sensing the same danger that I sense when my doctor crams his hand into a latex examination glove—the fiend made a desperate dash straight toward me and through my legs. A *Salmo trutta* variant of *mano-a-mano*.

The defunct net was hanging from my waist and dragging like a drift sock in the water; my left hand was sporting the inelegant mesh glove, making it useless for, well, just about anything; my right hand was holding the fly rod above my head, and the 8-foot bamboo buggy whip was bent in a near-complete circle down toward my crotch. Line was speeding through my legs in response to the trout's ascent toward its goal of kissing my clumsy derriere goodbye. I managed to swing one of my legs over the line and return to some semblance of a proper fish-fighting position. Despite the mesh mitten on my line-handling hand, I again closed my distance to the fish. Then *el toro* launched another charge through the legs of *el torero* and we repeated the whole crazy scene.

The fish and I shortened our distance one final time, though this time I feared it was the fish that had initiated the maneuver. My first seize of its tail held for about one second. My next grab lasted two seconds. My third stuck just as my footing failed but this time I hung on. I fell to my knees and found myself eye-to-eye with the fish whose silver body stretched twenty-eight inches from the tip of its tail to the tip of its nose. After a few clumsy photographs, I released the lake-run behemoth and moved to the safety of the shore lest the fish make another vengeful run at my knees. Both the Madonna and I were a tattered mess. Either, or both, would surely fall apart if we attempted another cast, so I declared that our day was done.

Now, when someone asks me where they can catch a big trout, I tell them to follow the oxygen. Unless they want to catch a really big trout. Then I tell them to head south and fish for bass in marginal water for trout.

Voelker's Nijinsky

I PROUDLY ANNOUNCED that I had finally bought a bamboo fly rod. "It sounds like you're sunk. Do you understand that this isn't just a bamboo rod, it's your *first* bamboo rod?" The pronouncement and query came from John Gierach who—while conceding that plenty of people have more skill with and knowledge about bamboo rods—once wrote that no one loves them more than he. I had been served an enlightened warning by a man who, himself, had been sunk for many years.

For the first few months with my first bamboo rod, I mistakenly believed that one would be enough. For in this rod I saw and felt the beauty and grace that John Gierach, and John Voelker before him, had foretold. But sometime in late January or early February, with over 6 feet of snowfall assuring that these would be the fishless months, a startling realization overcame me. In late May and early June I'd be fishing the Big Escanaba River, and, for that, I'd need a bigger rod.

"I want you to meet the guy who just built a rod for me," my friend and John Voelker's grandson Adam said while we were attending the Midwest Fly Fishing Expo in lower Michigan. "It's a replica of one of my grandfather's rods. I think you could use a rod like this on the big river." Adam picked up a beautiful walnut case, then motioned for me to accompany him across the floor of the convention center. When we reached the exhibit booth for Alder Creek Rods, Adam introduced me to Ron Barch.

In the same way that John Gierach's appearance epitomizes a fly fisherman, Ron Barch's appearance epitomizes a bamboo rod builder. He has the inquisitive eyes of a scholar, the caring smile of an educator, and the rugged but well-kept appearance of a craftsman. Not all bamboo rod builders look like Ron, of course, but Ron sure as hell looks like a bamboo rod builder.

In 2011 Ron was chosen by his peers to receive the A.P. Bellinger Award, which is presented annually to a rodmaker who best demonstrates that quality and integrity never go out of style. The respect the bamboo rod-making community has for Ron—and the respect Ron has for the bamboo rod-making profession—made him the natural choice when Adam wanted someone to measure and record the tapers for three of his grandfather's rods. Ron subsequently agreed to replicate one of the rods—a distinctive 8'6" three-piece 1928 Thomas with two tips that were restored by Paul Young—and that replica was in the walnut case in Adam's right hand.

"The casting pool is open," Ron said to Adam, and the three of us dashed through the main exhibit aisle to the pool. Once there, Adam assembled the rod, attached a reel, strung a line through the guides and began to cast.

"That rod casts much better than I thought it would," Ron whispered as we watched Adam cast. "I was afraid it would be a sentimental novelty, but you could fish with that rod."

Adam made several skillful casts. A few for short distance, several for long distance, then a few for very long distance. He finished with four or five of the roll casts his grandfather taught him forty or so years ago, and then called me to his side and put the rod in my hand. "Give it a try."

The rod was longer and heavier than my first bamboo rod. Apprehensive and nervous, my instincts took over and I began hauling and shooting line. "No, no. Let the rod do the work," came a polite, but firm, suggestion from Ron. "Close your eyes if you need to, then react to the rod. It will tell you what to do."

> *back . . . halt . . . wait . . . load . . .*
> *forward . . . halt . . . wait . . . load . . .*
> *back . . . halt . . . wait . . . load . . .*
> *forward . . . halt.*

The line straightened over the shallow pool and settled somewhere near the 60-foot marker.

"Wow," I said. "That's a fine rod. Would it be possible for you to make another someday?"

"I think so," Ron said.

"Could you make one by May 23rd? It's our 25th wedding anniversary, and I think my wife would like to give me a rod like this."

"Does your wife know that she thinks she would like to give you a rod like this?"

"Not yet."

Back in my office, still in Michigan but 550 miles from the Fly Fishing Expo, I pored over Adam's grandfather's books searching for references to the rod.

> *Like many another guilty trout fisherman, I own enough split*
> *bamboo fly rods to furnish buggy whips for most of the harness*
> *drivers of America. I posses at least one of every well-known*

40

*make and quite a raft of others by rod builders one rarely ever
hears of, possibly because many of them are dead and the rest
have more work than they can handle. And like the man with a
million ties on his rack, I usually "wear" only one, a gallant
and battered old three-piece number that was old before our
children, now grown, were even born.*

Anatomy of a Fisherman, 1964

*I still have several rods made by Paul Young himself (now
prized collectors' items) including one real oldie Paul used
himself, a weepy old Thomas that used to make me feel like
Nijinsky himself when I get waving it with a full head of line.*

Trout Magic, 1974

Nearly 25 years after Trout Magic and nearly 35 years after
Anatomy of a Fisherman, John Gierach wrote that "some of us
consider it an act of defiance to own something made by a dedicated
craftsman who may well be working as much for love as money and
who's proud enough of his work to sign it." Now, to enable my own
small act of defiance, a dedicated craftsman was performing his
craft in a Hastings, Michigan workshop. But as he would emphasize
through several correspondences over the next few months, Ron
Barch wasn't making a rod. Ron Barch was making my rod.

March 12:

Ron: *Have picked out the cane for your rod. Should get started
on it next week.*

Me: *I've been thinking about the rod lately (excitedly, I might
add).*

March 21:

> Ron: *Have your rod started.*
>
> Me: *Have my excitement started.*

April 1:

> Ron: *I have the strips roughed out and will begin the hand planing next week. With luck I believe I can make the May 23rd date. Do you want 2 different tips like the original, or should I blend the tips so they are a matching set? I am planning on a walnut cap and ring reelseat a touch heavier than on the original rod so as to have better balance.*
>
> Me: *Unless you see a serious problem with the original tips, I'd like to go with those for the tradition.*

April 9:

> Ron: *Will have your rod glued up later this week. Caught my first trout of the season Friday on a dry fly.*
>
> Me: *Hurray about the rod. Hurray about the trout.*

April 24:

> Ron: *I will be varnishing your rod this week.*
>
> Me: *Thanks for the update. I'm looking forward to casting and fishing with this rod.*

May 1:

> Ron: *Do you want your name on the rod blank?*
>
> Me: *No, I don't want my name on the rod. I think having something like "Voelker's Nijinsky", and anything else you think is appropriate (your name as builder, for instance) would be best.*

May 7:

> Ron: *We are down to the finish line. Rod is varnished and curing. You can have 3 choices of wrap colors: 1) Chestnut like on Adam's rod; 2) Medium brown which is kinda classic; 3) Hunter green which is what I use on most of my rods . . . sort of a signature color; or 4) anything else you really want, but these are my suggestions.*

> Me: *Let's go with your signature color.*

May 14:

> Ron: *I should have your new cane rod ready to ship by Friday. I really like the green wraps!*

> Me: *I am excited about this wonderful rod.*

May 15:

> Ron: *One more coat of varnish on the wraps and it's done. Have the walnut case drying and will put the finishing touches on everything tomorrow.*

> Me: *Thanks Ron. I hope we get to fish together some day soon.*

May 17:

> Ron: *I have just finished test casting your rod on the lawn and am happy to report that it turned out just as I had hoped. The light tip worked well with a DT 5wt and the second heavier tip cast a DT 6wt with authority. I cannot decide which tip I liked the best. Although I am leaning towards the heavier tip because of its power, the lighter tip cast a long delicate line. Both tips worked out to 60 ft. with no problem. Just make sure to slow down and let the rod load. This is an old design and that's the way the Judge wanted the rod to work. Will ship on Friday morning.*

Me: *Thanks for all of the effort you have put into making this rod. I am EXCITED to see it.*

May 22 (morning):

Me: *The rod arrived yesterday, and I was able to take it out for a few hours on a local river. It is a beautiful rod, and it casts wonderfully. I used the 5wt tip with a DT 5 line. I've attached a couple photos of the first two fish on the rod. Thanks again for a great rod. I'll keep you posted about its adventures.*

Ron: *I am probably smiling as much as you. The photos are magnificent and I am so glad to make a rod for someone who will use it.*

May 22 (night):

Me: *I'm glad to learn you are smiling. I went out again tonight (no fishing for about the next week, so I have to get out while I can), and got another nice fish on the rod. I've attached a few photos. On one hand this is a special rod that I want to protect. On the other hand, a big reason for getting the rod is to have a similar fishing experience as Voelker. So fish the rod I will. With each outing I am appreciating the wonder of this rod. It is a great wand.*

Ron: *Your photography rivals my rod making! May I share them with Mike McCoy the owner of Snake Brand guides? I used them on your rod.*

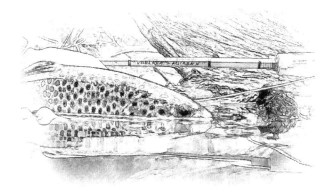

The rod stayed in its case for the next week. Then it was time for the big river. The Big Esky is over 100 feet wide in places, but its size alone isn't the challenge. Its current and bottom allow for easy wading, and a good caster can reach most of the fish with a 4 or 5 weight rod, provided that the wind isn't gusting strongly up or down the river. But the wind is nearly always gusting strongly up or down the river, and, when that happens, most 4 or 5 weight rods are overmatched. Voelker's Nijinsky was about to meet the river for which it was built.

I'd come to realize that aficionados could recognize a bamboo rod in your hand from a farther distance than they could recognize your face. What I hadn't come to realize yet was that some could smell bamboo from more than 20 feet. There is no other way to explain it. The man got out of his truck, walked to the back, opened his tailgate, cocked his head backward slightly, flared his nostrils and shouted "Hey, do you have a bamboo rod over there?" The rod was propped against the other side of my truck, well out of sight.

"Yes, I do."

"Mind if I take a look?"

"No, not at all."

"Wow. Whoever built this rod knew what they were doing. Look at those node placements. Perfect. Look at those wraps. Perfect. Do you mind if I cast it?"

The guy seemed to know what he was talking about, but he had the faint smell of alcohol on his breath. And Adam had warned that the only place a rod gets broken is between the tube and the stream. The tube was in my truck, and the stream was 100 yards away.

"Sure." I braced for the worst and thought about how I would explain this to Ron.

back . . . halt . . . wait . . . load . . .
forward . . . halt . . . wait . . . load . . .
back . . . halt . . . wait . . . load . . .
forward . . . halt.

Perfect. Far better than any cast I had ever made—or likely would ever make— with this or any other rod. A few more beautiful casts and he returned the rod to my hands.

"Tell Ron Barch he made one hell of a fly rod. And tell me the story of Voelker's Nijinsky."

I shared the story, shook hands with the man, then walked down the foot trail to the river. An old friend stood near the bank, looking upstream toward a spot where a small creek enters across from one of the few cabins on this stretch of river.

"A couple trout are rising between the cabin and the creek," he said. I'm not sure what they're eating, but another fisherman just gave up after casting for about half an hour."

"Go catch 'em." I said.

"I'm waiting for my son while I finish this beer. Why don't you see if Nijinsky is up for the task?" He had cast Nijinsky and learned its story about ten minutes before the man with the bamboo-smelling skills pulled into the parking area. I entered the river and keyed on a fish that was rising with a regular rhythm.

> *Sip . . . one-thousand one . . . one-thousand two . . .*
> *one-thousand three . . . one-thousand four . . . sip . . .*
> *one-thousand one . . . one-thousand two . . . one-thousand*
> *three . . . one-thousand four . . . sip . . .*

The only bugs on the surface or in the film were small and non-descript. I extended my tippet, attached a size 20 Griffith's Gnat, pulled some line from the Pflueger Medalist reel and prepared to cast. Two men walked along the bank behind me, and one saw—or smelled—the bamboo.

"Is that a bamboo rod?"

"Yes."

"Great. I'm fishing bamboo too. It's the only way to go."

The men walked on and I began to cast. Despite the miraculous lack of wind, my first offering was completely out of sync with the fish.

> *Sip . . . one-thousand one . . . one-thousand two . . . (fly floats*
> *by) . . . one-thousand three . . . one-thousand four . . . sip . . .*

My second cast was still poorly timed, but the third matched the fish's rhythm.

> *Sip . . . one-thousand one . . . one-thousand two . . . one-*
> *thousand three . . . one-thousand four . . . (fly floats by) . . .*
> *sip*

"That was great!" came a shout from the cabin just after I stopped the trout from its first long run down the river. The trout leaped and started its second downstream run. Voelker's Nijinsky held a delightful arc as it flexed to protect my 6x tippet. After a lively battle, I landed the fish just as the man from the cabin approached with a camera.

"Do you mind if I take a picture."

"No, not at all."

After he snapped a few photos, I released the fish and greeted my new friend. We chatted awhile, exchanged contact information, and the man offered to send the photos of me, Nijinsky, and the fish after he returned to his home in Minnesota. Then our conversation turned to the rod.

"So that's a bamboo rod?"

"Well, this isn't just a bamboo rod," my story began. "This is my second bamboo rod."

Sincerity

Sincerity—if you can fake that, you've got it made.
Attributed to many

THOSE OF US WHO relentlessly pursue large trout with a dry fly are hopeless addicts. If we weren't, we'd take up easy chores like curing cancer, ending world poverty, or explaining how long forever is. The essence of our addiction is not complicated. When we see a good trout rising, we don't simply want to catch it. We believe that we have to catch it.

But if we act on our urge to be the first to cast to every trout we see, we'll be bound to fish alone most of the time, and, regrettably, miss out on the delightful companionship of a good fishing buddy. To avoid this fate, many of us acquire and hone a skill that was first proposed and perfected by politicians. When it comes to negotiating the first cast to a good fish, we learn to fake sincerity.

When it comes to nearly everything else, though, a good fishing buddy rarely fakes sincerity. My friend Dave, for instance, always sinks a couple beers in a small feeder creek for us to drink on our walk out from the river. His generosity with beer is as sincere as his concern that a less sincere fisherman might pilfer a can, so Dave drinks Stroh's, and—although he won't admit it—I am convinced he does so to reduce the odds that someone will steal his beer. His son Brian drinks Hamm's for the same reason.

During a recent hike into one of our favorite spots, Dave said he hadn't fished this year. Not once. I'd already been out a couple dozen times, so when the first fish rose I suggested—with substantial sincerity—that Dave catch it, and he did. All eight inches. When another eight-inch fish rose he caught that one too. Sixteen combined inches of fish on two casts seemed pretty good to me, but, rather than risk twenty-four inches on three casts, Dave retreated to the bank and ignited a stinky cigar to fend off the mosquitoes.

Dave and I were chatting about past outings and fondly recalling a large fish he had hooked the previous year in this very spot. The river was substantially higher at that time than it was now. So high, in fact, that he and his boys and I had the river to ourselves, even though this is a popular place to fish during the brown-drake hatch. Because high flows scare away many of the other fishermen, we've come to enjoy the big water and what we call its *solitude-inducing* flows. We just look for the fish in different places, and learn to ignore the fish that are rising near the far bank. Except for the times when we feel bold, like Dave had the year before.

"Remember when you went after that fish across the river in the high flow last year?" I asked Dave.

"The one that David and Brian said I had no chance in hell of getting to? Yeah, I remember that one," Dave responded, with a wink.

Maybe he always intended to take a shot at that fish, but when the boys said he couldn't make it, there was no doubt that he would try. He took off his vest, put one box of flies in his shirt pocket, lit a cigar and waded upstream to launch his excursion. I'm pretty sure he floated at some point, though he wouldn't confirm or deny later that he had taken water in his waders. Once he'd made it through the deepest water and begun to ascend into waste deep water, he puffed some sort of smoke signal back to the boys and me. I don't know how to read smoke signals, but I'm pretty sure this one warned "bet against me at your own peril" or something like that. Then, of course, he caught the fish.

About the time we finished our reminiscence of Dave's exploits, another fish rose tight against the upstream bank. Its tiny body emerged from the water each time it rose for a fly, and we pegged it as a seven- or eight-inch fish.

"Your turn," Dave said sincerely.

Why would a fisherman who has spent thousands of dollars on rods, reels, clothing and flies use that equipment to cast for such a small fish? For the same reason, I suppose, that Wile E. Coyote spent thousands of dollars on Acme equipment to chase The Roadrunner, rather than simply spending a few dollars to buy some food. "I think you're missing the point here," Cliff Clavin once explained to Woody, Norm, and the rest of the gang at Cheers. "It's not that

Wile E. Coyote wants to eat necessarily, or that he wants to eat a roadrunner. What he wants is to eat that particular roadrunner."

Much like the hapless coyote, I didn't decide that I wanted to catch a small fish. I decided that I wanted to catch that particular small fish. So I slowly worked into position while Dave sat in the grass and smoked his cigar. Just before I made my first cast, though, Dave said that what we thought was the entire body of a seven-inch fish might, instead, be the nose of a much, much larger fish. It was.

Twenty inches of fish on one cast.

"Dave," I said after I had landed and released the fish a hundred or so feet down-stream, "this should have been your fish. I wish you would have caught it."

"No, Tim, I'm glad you got that one."

I'm sure we both sounded sincere.

The Good Old Days

I hate graveyards and old pawn shops.
John Prine

THE OLD MAN SAT IN A CHAIR next to the picnic table, which, to-day, was an impromptu bar stocked with a dozen bottles of whiskey. Most were bourbon, but one was an orange liqueur and another a fifth of Scotch that cost more than a decent pair of waders. The old man's assessment of the arrangement was simple. "Bourbon and other stuff that isn't bourbon."

A younger man crushed a small lump of sugar in a whiskey glass, added a dash of aromatic bitters, a jigger of bourbon, a few cubes of ice, and topped it off with some water and a slice of orange. He secured the drink in the old man's wrinkled hands and waited for the response. The old man loved whiskey Old Fashioneds.

"Delicious," the old man said with a wink. "Almost as good as the next one you'll be making for me." Today was the opening day of trout season, and the modest little fishing camp was overrun by men who had come to celebrate what the old man called "the first day." Some of the men were doctors or lawyers or other local dignitaries who didn't fish, but most fished at least a few times during the year.

The old man had been a splendid fisherman in his younger years, back before time stole his strength and mobility. Many years had now passed since he tramped through the woods and waded the rivers of his beloved Upper Peninsula, gathering mushrooms and gorging on wild berries in secluded environs known only to him. Now—on those rare occasions when he fished at all—he cast from a rusty old chair perched upon a rotting wooden platform on the shore of the camp's small spring-fed pond. And today, in the wake of a cold April morning, his arthritic fingers struggled just to hold his drink. But the younger man who'd made that drink knew that those worn fingers had killed or released more trout than most fishermen would ever see. For when the old man was the younger man's age— in his early fifties—he fished the local rivers and ponds harder and better than anyone.

The men in the group closest to the old man were exchanging lies about trout they hadn't caught and rivers they'd barely fished, when, in an unusual gush of honesty, one of the men declared that he hadn't caught a good fish in years. The reason, he asserted, was that the local fishing had gone to hell. Several others agreed that it was hardly worth going out.

"If the greedy loggers and miners have it their way, and the bureaucrats in Lansing keep looking the other direction every time some slithering lobbyist puts a dollar bill in their hands, then all our rivers will be completely ruined," one of the men said. "Hell, we might as well sit on our asses and drink all afternoon, then buy a few pounds of fish from the tribe and call it a day."

"Ain't that the truth?" the younger man said to the old man. "It must have been something to fish these rivers and ponds in the good old days."

The old man sat his drink on the table and pulled a small plastic box from the pocket of his shirt. He struggled to open its lid, then poured several colorful little flies into the palm of his hand. All the flies were a style that the old man and his friends called The Betty, although many fishermen would say they were Royal Coachman Trudes.

"The best fly I ever fished," the old man said. "I've caught more than half my fish on flies that looked just like these." Then he took another fly from his box and gave it to the younger man. It was a fly that most people would call an Adams.

"I hardly ever caught a fish on that fly. One of my worst flies," the old man said. But the younger man knew that the Adams was one of the most effective flies ever tied.

"Do you know why that fly was so bad for me?" the old man asked, then answered before the younger man could respond. "Because I rarely fished it. I didn't give it a chance. It sat in my box for years and I didn't know how wonderful it was because I didn't take it out, tie it on my line and fish it.

"The good old days you and the other men complain about are like the good old flies. You can have the greatest flies ever tied right there in your box, but it won't matter if you never take 'em out and fish 'em. It is the same thing with the good old days. Today, tomorrow and the next day could all be the good old days, but you'll never know if you don't go fishing. The good old days are when you can wade your favorite river without worrying that it might knock you on your ass and sweep you away. When you can see the tiny mayflies that float on the water, and watch the cedar waxwings snatch them from the air. When you can still hear the lonely bird sing its song. The good old days are happening right now for you boys, but you're leaving them locked in a big box of regret."

That was over thirty years ago. Now the younger man was an old man who sat in a bamboo chair while a crowd of younger men spread about the camp to celebrate another first day. Upon his request, I carefully prepared a drink, placed it in his hand and waited for the response. Then he told me his story about the good old days.

The Trout Will Let You Know

A FTER TED WILLIAMS WATCHED three pitches go by without offering the slightest evidence of a swing and the umpire yelled
"ball" each time, the young catcher behind the plate turned and
complained, "You're squeezing us, man."

"Listen, bud," the umpire responded, "when your pitcher throws
a strike, Mr. Williams will let you know."

Ted Williams was among the most potent hitters to ever play
major league baseball. His hand-eye coordination and physical skills
were superb, and he devoted nearly all of his substantial intellect to
the game. When the comedian Billy Crystal met Mr. Williams on the
field at Yankee Stadium long after the baseball icon had retired, Crystal told him that he had a thirty-year-old home movie of Williams
striking out against Crystal's beloved Yankees in the second game
of a double header, to which Williams replied "Curveball, low and
away. The catcher dropped the ball and tagged me, right?" He was
right.

Because Williams devoted so much of his mind to the game he
loved, the respect umpires gave to him was understandable. If he

didn't swing at a pitch, it probably wasn't a strike. It turns out that Williams was also a skilled fly fisherman, so it is likely that he gave the same deference to trout that the umpires gave to him. If a trout didn't take his fly, he understood, then it probably wasn't a strike.

That's what I thought about while I stood in the middle of the river and clipped off Clarence Roberts' Drake and replaced it with Ernie Borchers'. Clarence Roberts and Ernie Borchers aren't household names like Ted Williams, unless the household is in Michigan's Crawford or Roscommon Counties. There they might be, because the fly patterns they invented are sold in every fly shop around the Au Sable River system, and found in nearly every fly box on those rivers. Roberts' fly has a body made from deer hair and is usually tied with yellow thread so that it imitates light-colored mayflies. Borchers' fly has a body made from turkey quill fibers and is usually tied with black or brown thread so that it imitates dark-colored mayflies. With those two flies in small, medium, and large sizes you can fool most of the trout most of the time. But not all of the time. You are, after all, still fishing.

The night before I had used an odd little emerger pattern and caught every fish I put it over. Tonight was different. Tonight the trout ate all the flies on the river except for the ones on the end of my line, and this was the tenth time I had changed the pattern, the size, or both. Dave McMillan was fishing downstream and his story was the same. When another ring expanded just upstream, I turned and protested to the fish. *You're squeezing us, man.* Then I cast the Borchers and begged the fish to eat as the fly drifted toward its target.

"He took the Borchers! He took the Borchers!" I don't normally yell when I hook a fish, but I don't normally get squeezed like this either.

"Looks like a big fish," Dave said as the line sped off my reel.

"It's either big or foul hooked or both." I said.

After a couple long runs I realized that I'd hooked the fish in its side, so I tightened up to help the line break, but the trout swam straight toward Dave and he tried to land it. The fish rolled just when Dave made his move and the line snapped.

The next night I fished alone on the same stretch of river. About an hour before sunset the sky darkened from a colossal cloud of mayflies hovering in the air. Soon the water's surface was covered with the airplane silhouettes of dead mayflies, and the trout were eating them. I had a half dozen trout within casting distance, but I focused my attention on one that was staying just out of range. Everyone who fishes this river enough times will eventually encounter the same situation. A monster of a fish will surface like a porpoise as it gorges on mayfly spinners, rising perpendicular to the current while swimming in a seemingly random zig-zag pattern up and down the river. And, like me, they will ignore several good fish to tirelessly chase after the monster.

Like a purposeful worker on a production line, I cast my fruitless fly, let it drift over the fish, clipped it off, replaced it with another and did it again.

Cast, drift, clip, tie. Cast, drift, clip, tie. Cast . . .

The big fish ignored nearly all of my offerings, forcefully rising to devour a real fly just behind mine, just in front of mine, just to the left of mine, just to the right of mine, but never mine. Finally, when I offered an extended-body pattern that was smaller than the others I had been using, the big fish rose toward the surface in pursuit of my fly, then gently pushed my fraudulent offering to the side. *You're squeezing me, man.* Like a spurned lover on the rebound, I cast the fly toward the first other riser I saw, and that fish took.

With darkness descending, I hoped for a short scuffle so I could get back after the big fish, but, alas, the fight lasted longer than the light. With the fish finally corralled in my net and resting in the water, I removed the fly and reached for my camera. Then I noticed an odd growth on the fish's side.

> *Wait a minute, that's a fly. Not just any fly, that's a Borchers' Drake. Not just any Borchers' Drake, that's mine.*

"Listen up, bud," the fish said to me. "I know you think we're being unreasonable out here, but when you throw a strike, we'll let you know."

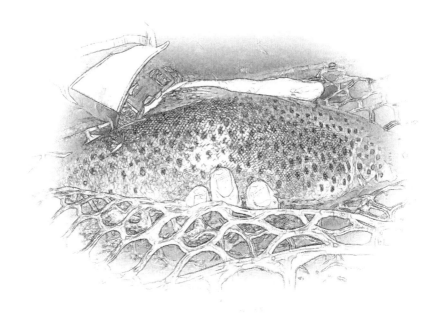

Jerry's Rod

M Y FRIEND ADAM—the same Adam who persuaded me to buy my first bamboo rod by pointing out that life is short and I could get run over by a moose tomorrow—began his note with a query that would have made my wife Roxanne's hair bristle had she read it.

Lusting after any new rods lately?

I took a long deep breath, loosened my collar, shut my office door, and then read on.

Jerry Kustich from Sweetgrass is retiring and selling a bunch of his stuff. You might want to see what he has left.

Jerry, it turns out, was gearing down for a momentous change in latitude, and, though Adam had already swooped up several, his list of available bamboo rods was impressive. What should I do? My bamboo arsenal had recently swelled from zero to three, which—according to a person whose hair had now begun to bristle—was already two more than any reasonable person should need. That was my answer, of course. Few people had mistaken me for a reasonable person, so I told Jerry I'd like to adopt two.

The first was a 7' 4-wt five-sided rod that Jerry had made as a prototype at Winston. Perfect for my local mid-sized streams. The rod came with two tips, and, later, after I broke one of the tips—somewhere between the case and the river, just where Adam had warned me that that sort of thing could happen—Jerry's colleagues at Sweetgrass made another that I have been careful to not break since.

The second rod was an 8' 6-wt Winston, which I believed would be an excellent complement to my existing rods on a big river like the Escanaba. The Escanaba flows through land that is as wild today as it was when John Voelker called it "a forgotten region which was virtually ignored in the westward surge of population," and as the river cuts and bends its way through the sprawling territory between Princeton and Cornell, it takes on a different personality in different places, so one rod isn't perfect for all parts of the river. I've been told that some bamboo fanatics will make up reasons for needing more than one rod for their favorite river, but this is not an addict's rationalization. A fly fisherman really does need more than one rod for this river. Really. And because the Escanaba is home to the Upper Peninsula's native bass and brook trout along with its alien brown trout, one of the river's splendors is that all of these fish can be caught with a fly rod, though not always with the same methods.

One side-effect of my transition from graphite to bamboo was a pronounced decline in my use of streamers and sinking lines. It's not that bamboo rods are incapable of flinging heavy lines with flies the size of small rabbits. Some are designed precisely for that purpose. It's just that stalking trout with a wooden rod and a tiny floating fly fulfills some deep personal yearning in a way that I have yet to completely comprehend. But I still haven't discovered a way to make trout rise on the Escanaba River—or any other river for that matter—when they don't want to rise. So, on a night when no fish were rising,

I attached a sink-tip leader and a rabbit-fur feather duster to the end of my line in a small act of self-assaulting irreverence. With a largely indifferent approach, I propelled the furry boat anchor across the river with the hope that Jerry's rod would—with some semblance of grace—ignore this feat of indiscretion and deposit the whole hairy mess in the general vicinity of a hungry smallmouth bass. One cast. One swing. One tug. One fish.

I rewarded the rod for its gallant service by clipping off the streamer and replacing the lead-core leader with 11 feet of knotted monofilament and a 5x tippet attached to a size 16 snowshoe emerger. I then plodded my way through the woods until I arrived at a favorite stretch of river and waited for a trout to feed from or just below the surface.

About an hour later it happened. The fish was at the tail of a small pool, picking off emerging flies with a regular rhythm. One cast. One drift. One tug. One fish. Like a non-judgmental old friend, Jerry's rod didn't care whether I was casting a four-inch-long strip of hair from the hide of a rabbit or a small tuft of fur from its foot. It simply did its job without complaint, just as if Jerry had designed it for this specific river.

I went back the next night without my lead-core leader and oversized flies convinced that this time I would catch a fish with a dry fly or I would not catch a fish at all. As it was in Voelker's day, access to most of the river without a boat or canoe is difficult at best and overwhelming at worst, and, about a fifth of the way into my odious hike, I found myself longingly obsessing about the difficult access. Because I'd be slogging out after dark, I tied strips of white garbage bag to branches in prominent spots along the way. The moon would be nearly full that night, so, with route-defining ribbons hanging from the trees and new batteries in my headlamp, I figured I'd be able to find my truck without the assistance of a herd of volunteer searchers accompanied by a "what on Earth has he done now?" reaction from Roxanne.

I emerged from my trudge into a section of river encompassing an alluring chain of riffles and pools. Part of my madness, though, is my willingness—nay, desire—to weather a prolonged battle with brambles and bushes only to watch over a fishy stretch of river as I sit on the bank flicking ticks and swatting mosquitoes while waiting for the rise of a lone trout.

At about 9 p.m. it happened. I didn't see the rise itself, just a small ripple radiating from the opposite bank. Two minutes later there was another. I suspected the fish was eating emerging flies, so I tied on a small snowshoe emerger—just like the one I had used the night before—and began a slow and deliberate march into the river. The fish was tight to the bank. A snag would most likely cause both the trout and the fisherman to mope and brood for the rest of the night. My first two casts were short. The third was on.

The fish swam first for deep water, then bolted toward a downed tree with a mess of amnesty-granting branches, but the rod did its job by simultaneously pressuring the fish and protecting the tippet. When I let the fish go, I felt relief in knowing that only one of us would mope and brood for the rest of the night. The other, the one with the million-dollar grin, would purr and beam and stumble clumsily from one impromptu route marker to the next.

As I began my dance toward the flag that marked my reentry into the woods, I thought about this beautiful rod that I probably didn't deserve, and I recalled the words that Jerry had written about his long relationship with a particular Martin guitar:

> *Although it was unlikely that my talent would ever be a worthy match, I was convinced of one thing: such a fine instrument would have the power to make a significant statement in a life searching for purpose.*

Maybe now was a good time to tell Roxanne that Jerry was selling some guitars too.

Small Stream Sisu

STEELHEAD ARE NOT NATIVE to Lake Superior. They have, however, made their homes in the great lake and its tributaries since the late 1800's, and in the minds of many local anglers, this fabricated fishery was designed as a simple two-stage process: put and take. For others of us, it's a more nuanced affair.

The states of Michigan, Wisconsin, and Minnesota each stock the lake's watershed with young rainbow trout. The State of Michigan, for instance, plants rainbows in nine of the Upper Peninsula tributaries of Lake Superior: about 100,000 seven-inch fish in the spring; about 500,000 three-inch fish in the fall. Many of these fish die before reaching the big lake. They are, after all, the perfect bite-sized treat for many of the pike, otters, hawks, and eagles that patrol those streams. Others, though, make it out to grow large and powerful in the dark depths of Superior, and one day they respond to a genetic force that tugs them back toward moving water. Some of those return to the place where they were planted, but the mavericks among them are drawn to creeks and streams they've never seen. Once there, they plant the seeds of a new generation. Those fish—the ones that are born according to a plan that didn't need approval from a horde of Lansing bureaucrats—are the ones that I adore.

Despite its natural beauty and allure, Michigan's Upper Peninsula is a harsh environment. The hardy men and women who lay roots in its towns and villages are in many ways similar to the authority-defying steelhead that populate its rivers. The motives for living in the U.P. are as diverse as the people who reside there, but if you needed one succinct explanation for why they are there, it would come from one of the peninsula's most accomplished natives. The *Life Magazine* photographer Bob Kelley once asked John Voelker what magical lure there was about trout fishing "that would make a presumably intelligent man, one endowed with a four-karat legal education, quit a more or less permanent job on the state's highest court to flee home to chase trout and write yarns about it?"

"Just lucky, I guess," the cagey judge replied.

Today, about 300,000 lucky people live in Michigan's Upper Peninsula. With about 18 residents per square mile, it's not as sparse as Alaska or Wyoming or Montana. Those states win with shear land mass. But the largest city in the Upper Peninsula has a population of only about 20,000, and the region is without question the most wild and remote in the Midwest. Being a Yooper might be lucky, but it's not easy. Living here demands a near-daily struggle with nature. We fight biting winds in the winter. We swat biting bugs in the summer.

Like many geographic regions of the country, part of the charm of the Upper Peninsula is the lingo its natives speak. Rugged immigrants from northern Europe and Scandinavia developed a dialect characterized by its accent on the first syllable and its tendency toward leading with the negative. Pauli breaks the pin on his snow blower and his day is *not so good*. Pasi scores four goals in the hockey league's championship game and his night is *not so bad*.

Of the many characters I've seen during my time living in the Upper Peninsula, John Syrgemaki is among the most memorable. In 1983, John shot a 400-pound black bear while hunting near his home on the eastern end of the Upper Peninsula. Still wearing a blaze-orange vest with the words

DON'T SHOOT, I AM A MAN

stamped across his back, John described his kill to a reporter from the region's lone television station.

"I was walkeen an hunteen deer when I come up on a gully-like and I stop to take a leak. Nature call, you know. So derit was . . . on a hill. And I thought what da hell is dat black one der? He start to move, so I move too, you know. In case like dat, you have'n got time to teenk. You do naturally what you supposed to."

"Well, that was pretty good luck, eh?" the reporter asked.

Squinting through dusty horn-rimmed bifocals, with his right hand loosely cupped beneath his unshaven chin, John grinned as he tilted his head in the direction of the dead bear hanging from the aluminum ladder behind him.

"Not so good for dis one."

The "why" of the U.P. can be hard to explain. I've often searched for the right words to describe the bond that Yooper's feel with their home, and my search always comes back to one Finnish word: sisu. Most translations of it miss the nuance, but Jerry Dennis got it right in his book The Windward Shore:

> *It is stoicism stripped of its philosopher's robe and dressed in a Woolrich hunting coat and a Packers cap, with a chainsaw in the back of the pickup and a snowmobile rusting all summer in the yard. It means sticking to a job until it is finished, no matter how difficult it is or how long it takes, and one of those jobs, the one that requires the greatest endurance and the most courage, is life itself. In a harsh climate and inhospitable land,* sisu *helps a person get by with dignity.*

So, what does sisu have to do with a wild steelhead—one that has yet to abandon the small remote stream of its birth to mature in the greatest of the Great Lakes? Look carefully when you meet one. The answer is in its eye.

Keith

TWO RECENT DEATHS in my family sent me searching through old boxes and files for a photograph someone took during a camping trip in southern Illinois sometime around 1970. My obsession worsened for about a month until the person most affected by those deaths sent me a scan of the photograph.

My cousin Bruce stood in the back of the photograph with his son Randy in his arms. Bruce's wife Charlotte—the person who sent me the photograph—was seated at the table in the lower right of the picture. Charlotte's grandfather, mother, father, and some of her parents' friends were standing next to Bruce and Randy. Bruce's mom—my Aunt Gladys—was sitting next to Charlotte. Next to Aunt Gladys was my mom, and next to my mom was my stepfather Cy. Across from Cy, at the far left corner of the table, was my mom's brother and Bruce's father, Uncle Floyd. My cousin Keith and I were seated at the table in the front of the picture.

Uncle Floyd is the man I most admired when I was a child. He went to Europe to fight in World War II, hunted and fished the way I wanted to hunt and fish, and made his living as a maintenance mechanic for Southern Illinois University. His smile was broad and contagious—the kind of smile that easily shatters cultural and class boundaries—so it was not surprising that, upon learning his last name was Holliday, many of the university professors respectfully called him Doc. Uncle Floyd raised a bountiful garden, and I remember that a biology professor would visit frequently to ask Doc for advice about gardening. Looking back, I don't think the professor really cared about gardening. He just liked to talk to Uncle Floyd, and Uncle Floyd liked to talk to him.

As a boy, I had limited relationships with men in general and father figures in particular. My father left before I was old enough to know him. My mom remarried a man named Jack Schulz whom I liked so much that I took his last name, but he died when I was six. She married my second stepfather Cy around the time of this picture, and, although I liked him at times, I could never get used to the yelling and screaming whenever he and my mom drank too much. They probably shared equal blame for the outbursts, but I never doubted whose side I was on.

Although my mom taught me to fish her way, over time I increasingly wanted to fish like Uncle Floyd and Bruce. Mom taught me to fish effectively and patiently with bait, but Uncle Floyd and Bruce fished excitingly and hastily with lures that they could cast and retrieve, over and over again. Mom wasn't much impressed with Bruce's method of fishing, but she believed he was the perfect example of how a young man should live his life, so she encouraged Bruce to take me fishing as much as possible. "Grow up to be like Bruce," she'd say, "and find yourself a sweet girl like Charlotte." I was only 19 when my mom died, so I don't know if she'd be satisfied with the way I've lived my life. But although she never met my wife, Roxanne, I am certain she'd approve of that part.

Uncle Floyd, Bruce, and Cy all influenced my life in important ways, but, lately, the person I've been thinking about most is the young boy who was in the lower left of the photo. That was my cousin Keith, and I was the kid with the sheepish look to his left. Keith was Bruce and Charlotte's first son, so, strictly speaking, he was my cousin once removed, but I've always just called him my cousin.

My relationship with Keith was different than with anyone else I knew in those years. We spent a lot of time together, but we didn't play the way I played with other friends. When we were stuck inside and bored, for instance, we'd do things like look through the J.C. Penney catalog. Like most boys my age, I'd be interested in the toys and balls and bikes, and maybe even the guns, but Keith would look at the clothes. "What do you think about this shirt?" he'd ask. "Looks okay," I'd respond. I didn't think kids were supposed to fantasize about new clothes, but I had to concede that it was kinda fun and the stuff that Keith said looked nice did, indeed, look nice. And while many of my other friends listened to music that I didn't like very much, Keith liked to listen to Elton John, and I had to admit that I did too. But when it came to spending time outdoors, we'd often part ways. I'd follow Uncle Floyd and Bruce around the yard and pester them to take me fishing, while Keith would stay inside and talk with my mom and Aunt Gladys.

On our drives home after a visit, Mom and Cy would talk about how something was different about Keith. Between swigs of Falstaff from a can that he'd wrapped in a paper towel so the police couldn't see that he was drinking beer in the car, Cy would say that it wasn't right for a kid to want to talk with the women so much. Mom would agree. I understood what they were saying, but, for me, the thing that stood out most about Keith was that he was the nicest boy I knew.

Keith and I saw each other less often as we grew older, and, after my mom died in 1981, I moved to California and we lost touch completely. When Uncle Floyd died in the early 90s, I flew back from Michigan and Keith flew back from Texas. After the funeral, I went with Keith to a riverboat casino to have a few drinks and play the slot machines. At some point in the night, Keith started laughing and said "I don't think we're having a few drinks anymore. We are *drinking* now." Later that night we sat on the kitchen floor in his parents' house and ate the food that was left over from the wake. We mostly joked and laughed, but Keith got serious for a while and told me how excited he was about President Clinton. "Timmy," he said, "I know some people don't think you should let one issue define your politics, but it's hard not to do that when that one issue is who you are and how you find happiness in your life." We both flew home the next day, and that was the last time I talked to Keith.

When the hospital Keith worked for "downsized" his job a few years ago, Keith and his partner Greg moved back to Illinois to be near Keith's mom, his dad, his brother Randy and Randy's wife Stacy. There, they'd be close to the people who loved them for the one issue

73

that Keith told me about the night of Uncle Floyd's funeral: who they were and how they found happiness in their lives. But when Greg—who had been Keith's life partner for 17 years—died last May, Keith's heart broke and he fell into a deep depression. Much of the happiness he had found was gone. Then, when Keith's father Bruce died a week before Christmas, his heartbreak and depression intensified. Two months later, Charlotte took Keith to the hospital with symptoms of pneumonia, and a few days after that, at 4 a.m. on February 14, Keith's broken heart stopped beating.

Hundreds of miles and decades of time were between me and Keith now, so I had to learn all of the details of Keith's last years from Stacy. And when she finished by saying that Keith got to be with Greg for Valentine's Day after all, I cried.

Atlantis Found

IN MARCH OF 2011, National Geographic aired a video in which a team of archeologists unveiled a series of clues they believed would uncover one of humankind's most controversial and elusive cities: Plato's Atlantis. Using ground-penetrating radars, an electrical resistivity tomograph, and advanced satellite imaging methods, the scientists poked around a muddy swamp gathering clues that they believed would transform Atlantis from a city of mystery to a city of history. At roughly the same time, but over four thousand miles away, I initiated a quest for a lesser known—but equally elusive— lost Utopia: the Upper Peninsula's Moose Creek and its fabled Camp Alice. Though my navigation was aided by GPS, satellite maps, and plat books, my most important guide was a dog-eared paperback edition of *Trout Madness* in which John Voelker's words from his story "Lost Atlantis" had served as the primary inspiration for my first quest to find the headwaters of Camp Alice and its "barrels of beautiful trout."

I launched my first excursion to Camp Alice on the opening day of Michigan's trout season. Although roads blocked by snow and padlocked cables thwarted my journey, I swore with the confidence and commitment of General MacArthur at Adelaide that "I came through and I shall return." But I would not return alone.

In late winter I sent several requests to friends and acquaintances for information and advice that might help with my quest to rediscover the environs that John Voelker described so delightfully in his books *Trout Madness*, *Trout Magic*, and *Anatomy of a Fisherman*. A friend responded and said he had forwarded my message to John Voelker's grandson, Adam Tsaloff. A day later I received a note from Adam: he didn't think he could provide new information about the locations, but he did know the man who wrote the stories, and he knew him well.

I told Adam about my project and about my work to date. He was interested, and suggested we meet during one of his subsequent visits to the Upper Peninsula. Two and a half months later I joined Adam and his good friend James Deloria at the place Adam's grandfather cunningly called Frenchman's Pond. The real name of the pond is not much of a secret nowadays, but it will always be Frenchman's Pond to me.

And so it was that Adam, James, and I began our expedition to Camp Alice. Our group's apparatus included a Garmin GPS for my truck, my iPhone's portable GPS, and an iPad loaded with electronic maps and plat books. We didn't have radars and tomographs like Professor Freund's squad, but we weren't searching for ten-thousand-year-old artifacts from a society that—according to Plato—sank into the ocean in a single day. No, we were simply looking for a creek and pond that an ambiguous angler had deceptively described in a fifty-year-old essay. This should be easy.

A cable and sign still blocked the road to Camp Alice, but the private road into the adjacent camp was open. What would it hurt to take a look? James is a big, strong man, and we had John Voelker's grandson in the truck. We should be able to talk our way out of any predicament short of a gunfight. But we were in the U.P., I thought, where a gunfight with trespassers is far from unheard of. Still, we drove on.

As we motored slowly toward the backwoods shack, I saw a head poke through the cabin doorway first, then a right hand followed by a left hand, neither of which held a gun. We waved, and the man walked out of the cabin and toward our truck. He didn't seem happy to see us, but he didn't appear to be too unhappy either. Still, I scanned the yard for the quickest escape route, and my right foot was in position and ready to drop on the accelerator if needed.

James spoke first. "Hi. We're trying to get into Camp Alice on Moose Creek. Can we access it from here?"

"Ya, dat's da Moose Creek. Whad you lewkeen for?" The man was standing next to our truck now, and his eyes were stunning. Electric blue irises surrounded by white scleras that were crisscrossed with blood-red streaks. His long gray hair was uncombed and in matted disarray from being constantly crowned by a red-and-black plaid Stormy Kromer, which he had just removed in some sort of backwoods gesture of etiquette.

"We'd like to do a little fishing, and we're looking for some of the places John Voelker used to fish. That's his grandson in the back seat." James declared.

The man responded, "Ya, he wrote one heez stories bout dis place. Dat one bout paddleen heez way up to headwaters. Dat was here. Feeshen better at dam. Not so good here."

"Is the dam up by Camp Alice?" I asked, pointing back toward the gated road.

"Ya."

"Do you know why they call it Camp Alice?"

"No."

"Do you think the owner would let us in there."

"No."

"Even with John Voelker's grandson?"

"No."

We thanked the man for his time and drove off for the public land on the other side of the pond. My previous attempt to get in had been derailed by late-season snowpack, but all the snow was gone now. We followed the road to its end, then set out on foot to find the creek and pond.

Our walk to the pond should have taken about ten minutes, but instead took nearly an hour. A confusing topography, a lack of trust in the iPhone GPS, and two conductors trying to drive one train caused us to plod our way through an unnecessary maze of windfalls and slash. We thought about giving up, but, as John Voelker wrote in the story that inspired this adventure, "there is no lunatic quite like a trout lunatic."

James first saw the sparkle of water through the pines, and we soon emerged on the shore of the pond near the middle of its length. The main dam was out of sight in one direction, and the narrow channel of Moose Creek was out of sight in the other. Adam and James began casting, and I began plotting my return with a boat. Once again I declared, "I came through and I shall return."

Mañana

W HEN I INTERVIEWED for a faculty position at Michigan Tech, my friend Warren—a guy I'd come to know for his uncanny knack for always looking like he knows what he is doing—shared an ominous warning: "To live here you need to think of April as a winter month, and it will help if you expect some snow in May."

Over the years that I've lived in Houghton since then the average snowfall in April has been more than nine inches, with more than thirty inches falling twice, and we've seen snow in about a third of the Mays. My friend Doug and I once caught 18 steelhead during a snowstorm on the first day of May swinging flies through a long run on the Huron River without once moving from our respective spots across from each other. My friend Cam and I once dug my canoe out from under a massive pile of snow on the fifth day of May only to find that the weight of the snow had pushed the bottom of the canoe to a position that was above the gunwales. We went into the house for a drink and listened to James Taylor sing "Carolina In My Mind," and by the time we returned the heat from the sun had coaxed the polyethylene material back into something close to its original shape, and I was able to use that canoe until it was destroyed by rapids the following year on an ill-advised float on the Middle Branch of the Ontonagon during the run-off from late April and early May snow storms.

With that history I should have been neither surprised nor disappointed when I awoke to a blanket of white in the middle of the so-called merry month, but I was both, and the lines from Jimmy Buffett's song Mañana echoed relentlessly in my mind:

> *She said I can't go back to America soon*
> *It's so goddamn cold it's gonna snow until June . . .*

I went to bed thinking I'd fish the next day, but with fresh snow and a forecast for temperatures in the thirties, I changed the date on my itinerary to Buffet's conveniently vague manna. Content to brood away the day on the couch, I browsed Facebook for inspiration and, perhaps, another voice to replace Buffett's. The first thing I read, though, was a proclamation by one of Michigan's finest writers and fishermen. "Trout love snow," Michael Delp wrote, and, with that, Buffet's chorus rang out in my head, and I sang along with an embellished harmony:

> *Please don't say Mañana if you don't mean it*
> *I have heard those words for so very long*
> *Don't try to* predict the fishing *if you've never seen it*
> *Don't ever forget that you just may wind up being wrong*

My mother liked to say that talking to yourself was not a problem. The only time for concern, she said, was when you started answering. Feeling like I was dangerously close to cause for concern, I aimed the truck south and drove toward Iron County. The South Branch of the Paint, Cook's Run, the Iron River and several other streams all host hatches of Hendricksons, and, much like Delp's trout, Hendricksons like snow.

The Hendrickson—or *Ephemerella subvaria* as it is called by so-phisticated piscators—is the first significant mayfly to hatch on Mid-western rivers. Unlike the larger mayflies that hatch near and after dark in June, this genteel fly does its business during a more reason-able time of day, sometime between lunch and dinner. Yet for all its refinement, this is not an entirely accommodating fly. You can—and if you do this enough, you will—spend hours staring expectantly at the water without seeing a single fly. When you hit it right, though, you will experience the birth of a new fishing season in the most glorious way it can be happen.

When the first sailboat silhouette floated by, my watch showed 2 P.M., which, even though I live at essentially the same longitude, is only 1 P.M. in Iron County's time zone. Another fly drifted past, then another and another and another, and soon the river was covered with fluttering flies. Not as thoroughly as the snow had covered the yard in the morning, but it was close. If I tossed a dinner plate onto the water, I'd surely hit three flies, probably more. But I hadn't come for the mayflies. I'd come for the trout that eat the mayflies, and I couldn't see any signs of that happening. A hoard of Hendricksons covered the river, but I didn't see a single rising fish. At least not where I was looking.

I first learned about the Hendrickson hatch from Jerry Dennis' es-say "Eight Days of Hendricksons." Every day from May 13 through May 20, Jerry faithfully returned to a riffle he called Red Cabin be-cause Kelly Galloup had once said, "Good Hennie riff. Big fish." I'm sometimes slow to learn things, even when—or sometimes especially when—those things should be obvious. The stretch of river I was fishing is a place where I catch trout throughout the summer months. A beautiful pool that flows gently between two riffle bends, the water is deep and shaded by a hardwood canopy. The bank is undercut. It is the ideal place to find a large trout sipping sulphurs or brown drakes at dusk. In something akin to an epiphany I realized that it wasn't summer, the flies were Hendricksons, and I should be looking for fish in the riffles. When I did, it happened just the way Jerry said it would:

> *The sun tries to break free, but clouds move in to cover it. When they do, the sky closes, the river opens, and my fly disappears.*

We Said We Were Going Fishing and We Did

I ARRIVED AT THE CROSSROADS shortly before 9:30 a.m., a full half hour before I needed to be there, so I had plenty of time to add ice to my cooler and fill my truck's tank with gas. I had driven all morning under the cover of an overcast sky, but now the clouds had cleared and the temperature was rising toward ninety. Catching a trout on an afternoon like this in a shallow spring-fed pond would be nearly impossible, but that didn't matter. This trip was all about people and place. On this bright and balmy June morning, I was escorting John Gierach into Frenchman's Pond.

With over twenty books on the topic, John Gierach is one of the most successful fishing writers of all time, and one of the best known fly fishermen in the country. Typically attired in a ragged button-down shirt, blue jeans and an iconic full-brimmed fishing hat, John surely looks like a man whose most popular book would bear the title *Trout Bum*. He injects his unique trout-bum philosophy into many of his stories, and one of my favorites involves an ordeal in which the tanks at a gas station that neighbored his home leaked gasoline into the ground and ruined his water supply. He sold his house to the station's parent company for the home's value before the contamination, plus a little extra for his trouble, and when his attorney suggested that they could get a million dollars in addition, John declined. The attorney said he had never had a client walk away from money, to which John replied that "most of us don't want money, we just want relief from the struggle for it," which was something he already had. When I told John how much I liked that observation, he shrugged a bit and said something like "thank you, but if you write as many words as I have, some of them will eventually come out right."

A week or two before John came to the Upper Peninsula, his friend Bill Bellinger had called the local fishing guide Brad Petzke and asked if Brad could take John fishing on the Escanaba River. Brad was fully booked with trips for Atlantic salmon on the St. Mary's River the week John would be in town, so he regretfully passed the opportunity to his good friend Matt Torreano. Mr. Gierach would be in good hands; no one knows the Escanaba River better than Matt. The week John arrived, however, relentless rains battered the Upper Peninsula, and the flow rate on the Big Esky tripled.

Matt and I talked about the predicament, and I offered to contact John Voelker's grandson, Adam Tsaloff, to ask if we could take Gierach to Frenchman's Pond. Although Adam couldn't make it to the Upper Peninsula to join us, he immediately agreed to my request and arranged for his uncle, Earnest "Woody" Wood, to meet me, Matt, John, Bill, and a young boy named Sam at Frenchman's.

John, Bill, and Sam were in the Upper Peninsula in search of Lake Superior's elusive coaster brook trout, but the rains that had transformed the Big Esky into a raging torrent had come with enough wind to spoil their first few voyages on the lake the Ojibwe call

Gichigami. When the weather cleared, John and his friends hooked and landed a few of the south shore's most mysterious and misunderstood fish, and, on one of their outings they met a member of the Huron Mountain Club and lucked into fishing the Salmon-Trout river with permission, which distinguishes them from any other person I know who has fished there.

Bill, John, and Sam pulled into the Crossroads parking lot at about the same time Matt arrived. After brief introductions, our plan was set. John and his party would ride with me into Frenchman's. Matt had another commitment in the early afternoon, so he would follow in his truck. I suggested we stash Bill's truck near the township's small community garage, where an old snow plow, a retired school bus, and a beat-up tow truck were scattered throughout the gravel- and grass-covered lot. Bill asked if it was okay to park there, and, to be honest, I didn't know. I was, however, relatively sure that if and when the township towed a vehicle for illegal parking, this was the place they brought it. Either way, Bill's truck would be there when we returned.

John, Bill, and Sam loaded a few rods and other equipment into my truck, and we started off for the pond. The group seemed uneasy at first, and when I asked if everything was okay John replied that he thought they would need to be blind-folded before I escorted them into this secret and sacred place.

For all of its secrecy and mystique, hundreds of people have had the good fortune to visit Frenchman's Pond. Voelker and his family have generously escorted many friends and acquaintances into this shrine, and—though the property is clearly marked with signs inviting you to "keep the hell out"—many people have made private pilgrimages into the camp. Most have left without leaving a trace of their presence, though a few scoundrels have felt compelled to steal souvenirs. A fisherman stealing from Frenchman's is like a

Catholic stealing from the Vatican. For some, I suppose, decency is as delicate as an 8x tippet.

The long and tortuous road that leads to Frenchman's reaches a local crest on a rocky ridge just above the modest cabin. Once there, I parked my truck in a small clearing adjacent to a sign that proclaimed this to be a Bamboo Zone. "I'd like a photograph of this to show A.K.," John announced as he strolled toward the sign. Since he first began fishing with an 8-foot, three-piece, 7-weight Ed M. Hunter bamboo fly rod, John Gierach hadn't needed placards or signs to tell him that every pond, river or lake that he fished was a *Bamboo Zone*. Under normal circumstances, I suspect that John would have moderate-to-severe disdain for a sign that instructed a person how they could or could not fish. This, however, was not a normal circumstance.

Voelker's son-in-law Woody was fishing on the opposite side of the pond when his dog enthusiastically announced our arrival. Like most ancient beaver ponds in Michigan's Upper Peninsula, it is nearly impossible to wade this pond or hike along its shore. To enable moderate access to the pond, however, Woody has diligently maintained a network of foot trails and casting platforms around the pond, and, to provide access to both sides of the pond, he built and installed a replica of the original foot bridge that Voelker and his friends had stationed there many years ago.

After polite and friendly introductions, John and Woody began a delightful affair of bamboo show-and-tell. At some point Woody assembled a refurbished rod that Morris "the Rodmaker" Kushner had made for Judge Voelker, and we all sensed a special moment in the making as Woody handed the rod to John. John respectfully admired the craftsmanship and history of that historic rod, and, after Woody rigged the rod with a reel and line, the rest of us watched quietly as John walked down to the pond's dock and began to cast.

After John finished casting the Kushner rod, Woody graciously served a lunch of sausage, cheese, crackers and wine. Everyone knew at least one common friend or acquaintance, so, without the pretense of name-dropping, we shared a few stories about rod-builders, writers, and guides. Then it was time to fish.

John Voelker wrote about fishing on days when

> $\cdots$ *the surface of the water possesses a peculiar gun-metal sheen, a kind of bland, polished, and impersonal glitter, a most curious sort of bulging look, coupled with the aloof, metallic quality and cold, glassy expression of a dowager staring down a peasant through her lorgnette.*

An on those un-special days the Judge advised that we might as well leave our "rod in the case and instead go chase butterflies." This was one of those days, but we fished anyway, and left the butterfly chasing for Woody's dog. John walked to the dam, took off his boots and socks, rolled his jeans up to his knees, and waded a few steps into the pond's muck. He could easily cast across the pond by standing on dry land, so I think he did this to touch the ghosts that live in that fabled water.

As the temperature rose into the 90s, Woody caught the only fish of the day while casting from the dock in front of the cabin. And though John Gierach didn't catch a fish, he did declare the outing a great success. As we loaded the truck to leave, John looked at the water, flashed a smile of satisfaction, and reminded us of the wise pronouncement of his good friend A.K. Best:

> *We said we were going fishing and we did.*

How to Catch the Biggest Brook Trout of Your Life

I DON'T NORMALLY do how-to essays. My way of doing something might not be the best for everyone, so I worry about feeling bad when someone points out that there is a better way. Just the other day, though, I caught the biggest brook trout of my life. That made me feel good. Really good. And now that I've had some time to think about how it happened, I believe I know something so important that I have to share it.

Now, if you have caught at least one brook trout, then you have already caught the biggest brook trout of your life. I understand that. I want to tell you how to catch the biggest brook trout you will *ever* catch. Unless you have fished—or will fish—somewhere like Labrador. If you get to do that, then you don't need my help.

You can't do this alone, so the first thing you need to do is select a fishing partner. This can't be a person you've fished with before, so you'll have to arrange an outing with someone you haven't met, or at least haven't fished with. It really helps to find someone who likes IPA beers. Someone like Tom Hazelton.

Tom is an outdoor writer who lives in Minnesota. We got to know each other through our internet writings, and at some point we followed up on our "we should fish together someday" assertions and agreed to meet and fish for a couple days when Tom was passing through the Upper Peninsula, which is an unusual event in itself because few people have a reason to pass through the Upper Peninsula. It's not really on the way to anywhere.

Next, you should pick a place that you're familiar with, but that your new fishing partner is not. It's important that your friend believes that any stream or pond or lake you lead them to holds some nice brook trout. And it really helps if your destination is a beautiful place that your accomplice would like to fish regardless of whether or not they catch a fish. They need to be enthusiastic about fishing at this place.

The next step might not be an intuitive one, but it's critical. You need to make it seem as though the outing is all about your new fishing partner catching a nice fish. So don't even bother stringing up your rod at first. Just show your friend the best spots, then slip away to take a few pictures of flowers. This is also a good time to drink one of your friend's IPAs.

It is essential that you leave your friend alone. That way they will fish for a while in the places you suggested, then make the important decision to try some new spots on their own. Think about it. If you were going to catch the biggest brook trout of your life in one of the places you know about, you'd probably already have done it.

When you finish drinking your friend's IPA, go ahead and string up your rod and open another of your friend's IPAs. Take some more pictures of flowers, then work your way back to the water and make a few casts. At this point you're not trying to catch a fish. You're just practicing. Remember, you've had two of your friend's IPAs and you need to be sure you can get off a good cast when the time comes. So practice your casting.

By now your friend will have tired of fishing at the places you suggested, so they will have moved and won't be easy to find. When you do finally find them, they'll probably be releasing a fish. Be sure to act surprised, but not too surprised. Being charitable and kind, your friend will invite you to come and fish with them, but don't go just yet. Hold back until they catch a few more fish, then work your way into their spot. You need to be careful, though. You've had two IPAs, and you will need to crawl through some brambles or wade through some muck to get into the place your friend has found for you. It won't be easy to get in there because, if it was, you'd already know about it.

When you get to the spot, don't tell your friend that you drank two of their IPAs. They probably won't care, but you are too close to catching the biggest brook trout of your life to risk blowing it over a couple beers. Tell your friend how cool it is that they found this spot, then wait for a trout to rise. It won't take long. When the fish does rise, your friend will tell you to take a shot at it. Tell them that they should go for it because they found the spot. Don't worry, they will insist that you try for the fish.

Work out some line, take a deep breath, then make your cast. But don't screw it up. This may be your only chance to catch the biggest brook trout of your life.

It's About Time

> *How did it get so late so soon?*
> Dr. Suess

I N THE TIME IT TAKES our planet to complete an orbit around its sun, my friend Mike Sepelak goes fishing at least 52 times. More often if possible, but he's set the bar at an average of once a week. I met Mike because of his writing on a blog called *Mike's Gone Fishin' Again*, and, with a title like that, my only surprise about the frequency of his fishing was that he didn't fish more.

Because I was spending the academic year on sabbatical in North Carolina, I contacted Mike and he generously invited me on a few of his outings. Many of his trips are well-planned and researched, but his goal-securing outing for that year sprung from a simple invitation.

"I'm feeling itchy. Perhaps a quick trip early next week?"

"Please, and thank you," I replied.

With seven days in a week, fishing 52 times a year should be easy. But it's not. We fritter away hours, squander days, and unwittingly populate our past with fishless week after fishless week. Father Time is a heartless scoundrel who steals with impunity, and we carelessly neglect to lock our doors. For those of us residing above the 45th parallel, the situation intensifies when our rivers vanish below an impenetrable floor of ice and snow for months at a time. And if we get little solace from chugging shots of Red Bull and Jagermeister while dangling a frozen line through an eight-inch hole in the ice, then we're left with two options to cope with the endless winter. Brood and pout, or migrate south for the season.

After brooding and pouting for more than twenty years, my migratory home for that winter was about eleven degrees of latitude below—and more than thirty degrees of temperature above—my usual residence. So when Mike and I met the morning of our trip to the river, I wore a thin fleece jacket and a thick wide smile. Mike wore the same. We'd drive for two hours, he said, fish for six or seven, and then drive home. I had fished only once in roughly three months, so I hoped to devour those six or seven hours and leave little for Father Time to nab.

We parked in a small clearing near the river where we were promptly greeted by two overweight Labrador retrievers. The dogs knew Mike from his many previous trips, so they enthusiastically volunteered to accompany us for the next four or five hours, presenting their watchful eyes and intimidating snarls as safeguards from the wild creatures that prowled the woods. In return for their services, they asked only that we provide an occasional pat to their heads with a few comforting words spoken in their general direction.

When we arrived at the river, Mike put me on a fishy looking pool and waded downstream to swing streamers through a swiftly flowing run.

"Any advice on what I should do?" I asked.

"Fish for trout," Mike replied.

I didn't know much about this river, only that it was a tailwater and that the fish would likely feed on tiny midges. So, naturally, my first fish came on a size 18 bead-head pheasant tail, a fly that I used only for the purpose of getting the trailing size 20 midge down to the trout. Another reminder that if and when I select the right fly, the trout—and only the trout—will let me know. I released the fish and snuck a quick glance at my watch. It was noon. Father Time had already seized a couple hours, and if I didn't turn up my game, that merciless bandit would undoubtedly steal more from this glorious December day.

I fished steadily for another hour, then noticed Mike ambling along the bank behind me on his way upstream.

"Without looking at your watch, what time do you think it is?" I asked.

Mike glanced toward the sky. "I'd say it's noon."

"One o'clock," I sighed.

"That's later than I thought. We better keep casting."

Mike waded into some faster water and motioned for me to follow. A little later he spotted a pod of rising trout in a foamy eddy along the far bank and guided me into a perfect position across from the fish. I asked for advice and, once again, he suggested that I "fish for trout."

Most of the fish I'd seen that day were between 8 and 10 inches, and I had no reason to believe these were different. Regardless of the size of the fish, however, the margin for error with a size 20 or smaller dry fly is slight. In my probability class, I teach my students that if you toss a coin enough times, you can eventually see eight, ten, fifteen, twenty or more successive tosses showing tails. You just need to be patient and persistent. And so it is with me and tiny flies.

"Damn, it's dragging again," I blurted as the tiny fly seemed to skate near the end of its drift. Just then, though, the fly disappeared beneath a voracious rise, and the fish bolted for deeper water. "Or drifting perfectly," Mike responded as he snapped his net from its magnetic clasp.

After releasing the trout, I realized that Mike had netted a fish for me on only our second outing. Was it too soon? Was our relationship ready for such intimacy? We did have much in common. We used the same waterproof camera. We owned the same St. Croix rod. We were both compelled to check and recheck the truck's locks twice before walking away. It was the right time.

Mike looked at his watch. "Tim, what time do you have now?" he asked with a hint of skepticism. Then it hit me. The last time I wore my fishing watch was five days before legislative decree had obliged our clocks and watches to fall back one hour. So, as I joyfully spun my watch's crown to recoup the precious hour I'd lost, the ebullient overweight retrievers howled with delight. And somewhere in the distance—far beyond our guard dogs' perimeter—a deflated Father Time angrily cursed his loss. Mike and Tim had another hour to fish.

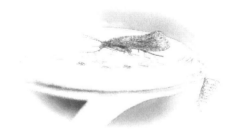

A Fish Called Dave

Non semper ea sunt, quae videntur; decipit
Frons prima multos.
Phaedrus
Book IV, Fable II

"HAVE YOU NAMED IT YET? I'd be honored if you'd name it Dave because I feel like I know it now, too."

Dave Delisi from Sweetgrass Rods was alluding to a brown trout whose allure was swiftly eroding my already meager capacity for self control. What makes one fish stubbornly reject a fly that another will eagerly take? How does the quest for an answer transform an otherwise capable man into a neurotic ninny?

"I'm concerned that the Siren song of Dave may be too much for me," I responded. "Tonight I'm putting beeswax in my ears, tying myself to the deck, and forbidding my family from untying me no matter how loudly I might beg." My Siren was a brown trout that I now called Dave, and my Tyrrhenian Sea was a remote river somewhere in the Ontonagon watershed.

The Ontonagon watershed spreads over 1,300 square miles in the Upper Peninsula of Michigan and Northern Wisconsin, a wilderness in which whitetail deer outnumber people 2 to 1. The Middle, South, East, West and Cisco branches do most of the work, but scores of smaller creeks with names like Caddis, Cedar, Clay Bottom, Imp, Jug, Jumbo, Kostlenick, Mile And One Half, New Home, Snuffbox, Sucker, and Whisky Hollow carry water for the drainage. And, of course, there is a Trout Brook and a Trout Creek. Many of these brooks, creeks, and rivers carve their tea-colored paths through the Ottawa National Forest, and most of the wild inhabitants that prowl this territory die natural deaths without ever seeing, hearing or smelling a human. It is here, in a spot where the slow flowing water of an undisclosed branch gently messages its alder-lined bank, that a fish called Dave patiently lingers, waiting to ambush the next helpless bug that perpetrates an ill-fated float through his dining zone.

It was early June, and I was breaking camp and heading homeward after a week on the Escanaba River. The trip had been a trifold success: good friends, good food and good fishing. I was well-worn and ragged, but still somehow restless and hesitant to let go. The direct route home—through Rock, McFarland, Gwinn, Ishpeming, Nestoria, and L'Anse—would weave its way through and around much of the Escanaba watershed and along many of the rivers I'd fished for the past week. The long route home—through Felch, Crystal Falls, Iron River, Bruce Crossing, and Twin Lakes—would add 50 miles to my journey, but, more important, wind its way through the heart of the Ontonagon drainage. My new bamboo rod— "Voelker's Nijinsky"—had excelled on the Esky. Now I would test its mettle on the Upper Peninsula's other big river.

Though much of the Ontonagon system flows through public land, access to the best locations is tricky. If you are ambitious and brave you can park fairly close to the river, but, when a seemingly small puddle becomes a bottomless pit of tire-grabbing goo, a five-mile walk for help will erode your ambition and blunt your bravery. Lessons like this need only be learned once, so I parked on high, safe ground and initiated a short but spirited hike to the water. I assembled the rod, attached the reel, strung the line, sat on a log and waited for a fish to announce its location.

The first rise radiated from under a weathered sweeper whose white branches and bark stood in remarkable contrast to the surrounding green foliage. I attached a Roberts Drake to my leader—a fly I've come to believe should be standard issue in all backwoods emergency survival kits—waded into the water and began to cast. Irksome current seams and eddies dragged and jerked my fly on every drift. On my one nearly drag-free cast, the trout rose just when the fly dragged. The surface erupted as the fish recognized my fraud and bolted for the bottom. I repeated this unproductive maneuver with two other fish, then returned to the log to mope and pout.

Another fish rose farther downstream. The rise was soft and subtle, so I grudgingly removed the Roberts Drake, downsized the tippet and attached a size 20 Griffith's Gnat. Two casts and I was on. Voelker's Nijinsky sprung to duty and proved its worth on another of the Upper Peninsula's big rivers. Though I had missed the larger fish, the summer had just started and if gas stayed below five dollars a gallon I could afford to return a few more times.

During the drive home my mind replayed those failed encounters with the bigger fish. I had caught a good fish. A very good fish. But the one I missed—the one that discerned my offering as a sham—was a great fish.

"Don't you think that you obsess a little too much about trout fishing?" Roxanne asked the following day while I paced the house like a caged tiger.

"Not at all. I only obsess about it when I'm not fishing."

Coincident with my reply, the early summer humidity caused her hand to lose its grip on a skillet, which, in turn, caused the skillet to take flight and narrowly miss my head. We agreed it would be best if I left the house until the humidity dropped to a safer level, so I bolted for the Great White Whale—an eighteen and a half foot Ford Expedition stocked with fishing equipment and enough food and drink to stave off hunger and thirst for a week.

Nearly two hours later I was sitting on my log staring at the sweeper when the large fish began to rise. Voelker's Nijinsky was a healthy scratch; in its place was my first bamboo rod, a 7'9" Sweetgrass Mantra. I attached a 3-foot tippet to compensate for the seams and eddies, tied on a Griffith's Gnat and put a well timed cast directly over the fish.

The tiny fly didn't drag and the trout ate. The fish bolted for the opposite bank, then turned left and drove into the current. The bulk of my line was still extending toward the opposite bank when the brute jumped for freedom 20 feet upstream. With so much line in the water I had no chance. *Ping.* My fly-less line had six inches of tippet attached to the leader. At least it wasn't my knot.

I had driven a long way for a shot at that fish. Now it was over. I sat on my log, tied on a new tippet and decided to wait another half hour. Ten minutes later a fish rose just below the sweeper. I attached a Gnat, carefully waded into position and caught the fish. An unknowing observer might have believed I knew what I was doing. Another good fish, but, alas, not the great fish I was after.

I feigned sanity and stayed away from the river for four days, but the pangs of obsession finally loosened my grasp on normalcy. That, and Roxanne's sympathetic encouragement: "For the sake of all that is precious about our family, you should go back to the river and try to catch that fish." Or something like that.

100

My third excursion to the river was much like the first. I hooked and landed one good fish, but the largest fish prudently refused my offerings. Three trips to the river and all I could claim were three unremarkable fish. Three good fish, to be sure, but the biggest fish—the one for which I had spent over $40 on fuel for each round trip—had eluded me.

I enjoy sending Dave photographs of fish I catch on the Sweetgrass rod, and Dave enjoys seeing them. I had already sent a snapshot from four nights earlier, and in the process of cleaning up the most recent photo, it struck me. The freckle patterns on the two fish were identical. They were the same fish.

"Got out again last night. I'm sure none of the Booboys (and girls) will be surprised by this, but catch and release and catch again does indeed work. Here is the star of my previous photo, as he looks four nights after the first photo shoot. I've done this a few times before, and each time I make a pledge to not catch the fish again. You kinda get to know 'em, and it breaks my heart to think of anything happening to a fish I've caught once or twice. I'm sentimental that way."

"Wow . . . you must have been using the same fly?"

"The same pattern, but a different fly. Those size 20 Griffith's Gnats don't stand up to too many fish. I have a confession to make about this fish in particular, and about my bamboo fly rods in general.

"I've been searching for the right way to tell you this, but I suppose the best way is to just say it: I bought another bamboo fly rod this year, and it is not a Sweetgrass Rod. I hope you can forgive me for succumbing to the enthralling lure of another rod. I was seduced."

At this point I reexamined the photo of the fish I had caught with Voelker's Nijinsky and continued my confession. "And, beyond that serious indiscretion, I unintentionally violated my catch twice rule with this fish. Last Friday I caught the fish with Voelker's Nijinsky. It turns out that the fish I caught on Saturday with the Mantra was the same. A few other nice fish had been rising, so I returned last night. I caught the fish again in a slightly different part of the run thinking it was one of the other fish. Several other fish feed (much more sporadically) in this run, so I've been returning with the hope of finding one of them rising in a steady—and catchable—pattern.

"So here are my confessions: first, I violated my rule and caught this fish three times; and second, I cheated on you with another rod. I hope you can forgive me."

"Not much time to respond," Dave began, "but first, know that I forgive you your cheating on me with another rod . . . I would consider ours an open marriage, Newt-Gingrich-style.

"Regarding catching the same fish three times, I think it is amazing and also a testimony to your gentle handling of the fish."

Still obsessed by the hope of catching the great fish under the old white sweeper, I returned to the river two weeks later. My note to Dave told the story:

"I went out tonight with the 4/5 Mantra. Caught a nice brown early in the evening, then went to a familiar section of the river. Four good fish were rising, and I targeted the one I thought was least likely to be the one I've caught three times this year. Well, this is getting out of control. As you can see, I caught the fish on a different fly (the most excellent Roberts Drake), but this is getting crazy. Some very nice fish live in this section, but I'll be darned if I don't keep catching the same fish. A fish rose in the spot where I'd caught this one before, and this fish was feeding twenty feet upstream, so I really believed I was onto a different fish this time. The trout swam away with gusto, though, so I guess I'm not hurting it too much. I honestly don't want to catch this fish anymore, so I may have to stop fishing that section of river."

"You crack me up," Dave replied. "I can just imagine your surprise each time you land the same freakin' fish. Have you named it yet? I'd be honored if you'd name it Dave because I feel like I know it now, too."

Things are not always what they seem;
The first appearance deceives many.
Phaedrus
Book IV, Fable II

Growing Older but Not Up

MUCH OF THE FUN of getting to know a new fishing buddy is the slow and pleasant process of asking questions about their life and answering questions about yours.

Where'd you grow up?

What do you do for a living?

If you could have any superpower, what would it be?

That's the routine Tom Hazelton and I were working through during our first trip together when he asked a question I didn't expect.

"Are you retired?"

Retired? I suppose I'm old enough to have children Tom's age, but for that to have happened I'd have had to muster the courage to speak to a girl—any girl—in high school, and because I didn't develop that particular superpower until I'd made it through four years of college, both of my children are much younger than Tom.

Early middle aged? Maybe. *Retired?* No.

In fairness to Tom, this wasn't the first time I'd been mistaken for an old guy. The AARP once sent an invitation for me to join their association, but only because some anonymous bureaucrat had mistakenly put my name on their list of old people. Tom's mistake was different. He was standing next to me and could see the same young man's face I see when I look in the mirror. Ragged old Filson hats must make early middle-aged men like me look older.

About the time I'd recuperated from Tom's question, I met a young man named Elliot who follows my writing and knows the rivers I've written about at least as well as—and probably better than—I know them. I'd been on the river for six straight days, and two cold fronts had shut down the fishing for most of that time. If Elliot saw me struggle through another fruitless evening, he'd surely peg me as a fly fishing writer who can't catch fish. Like a hockey player with a full set of teeth, a pirate with two good eyes, or a politician who can't lie, I'd be exposed as a fraud.

Hoping to dodge such an embarrassing unmasking, I snuck off to a wide section of the river where I crossed, hid in the woods, and wished for a good fish to rise. I uttered a few prayers too, and just when the sun dropped below the treetops and the last of its rays were off the water, the big-fish gods answered my pleas. A throng of huge trout rose, and I caught them all. The river was my canvas, the rod was my brush, and I painted a masterpiece. Luck smiled and I smiled back. Eight trout in less than two hours, and all were seventeen inches or longer. It was by far the best evening I'd had all week, and one of the best I'd had in my life.

Two guys were fishing downstream from me, and one of them was Elliot. I had just bought a new Hardy reel, and if you are familiar with the sound a Hardy reel makes when a fish pulls line against its drag, then you will understand that Elliot knew how many fish I caught and how long it took to land each one of them. Hardy,

I suspect, uses the same sound technology in their drag systems that Honeywell and other companies use in their fire alarms. They are designed to be heard. The following day I was surprised and delighted to receive a kind and thoughtful message from Elliot:

> *Hey Tim, it was great to meet you yesterday. Had a fun time chatting, and fun to watch you work your magic on those fish! I take comfort in the fact that 5 years of fly fishing experience is nowhere near enough to master it, and if I stick with it, someday I might be the old guy across the river slaying the fish on a bamboo rod!*

Old guy?

"All this 'old guy' and 'are you retired?' stuff is starting to piss me off," I wrote to my friend Jerry Dennis, and his quick reply endorsed my position.

> *I know. I'm getting pissed off too. Especially because just a year or two ago I was the guy looking across the river at the old man (sixty!) and thinking how great it was that he could still get around at his age.*

> *I hate to tell you, old friend, but it gets worse. Not long ago I went to a coffee shop and the tattooed, 22-year-old hipster counter jockey said, "What can I get you, young man?" I dove over the counter and throttled him until he was unconscious, wrote "I Am a Condescending Shit" on his forehead with a marker pen, and stole his wallet. Young man, indeed.*

I suppose old guys like Jerry and me can hold off the inevitable by throttling innocent hipsters or trading our fedoras and vests for trucker hats and backpacks, but eventually we'll have to concede that ten, twenty, or thirty more years have gotten behind us. The gray hairs, receding hairlines and aching knees are awkward—and obvious—reminders of your evolution from whomever it was that you once thought you were into that old guy across the river. Time is a good teacher, though, and if you keep your eyes open along the way you can learn a few worthwhile lessons. Assuming, of course, that you wear a good pair of corrective lenses to compensate for your diminished vision, and you make a simple five-point list so you don't forget.

1. *Short casts catch more fish than long casts.*
   If you want to get closer to something that is precious, shorten your shadow, soften your steps and weaken your wake.

2. *You're only as strong as your weakest knot.*
   If you don't want to lose the catch of a lifetime, check your knots twice. Then check them again. They are are the only things that keep you connected.

3. *Don't leave fish to find fish.*
   A bird in the hand is worth two in the bush. The grass is rarely greener on the other side. You know, that sort of thing.

4. *Don't be afraid to change flies.*
   Loyalty is important, but you'll miss many opportunities if you are unwilling to change.

5. *You can't fix a fouled leader with more casting.*
   When you're in a hole, drop the shovel. Stop doing the things that caused the problem in the first place. Random yanks on the line will just worsen the mess.

Of course Tom, Elliot, and the tattooed counter jockey are right. Jerry and I have grown older, and, I hope, a little wiser. But that doesn't mean we have to like it. And it sure as hell doesn't mean we have to grow up.

The Greenhorn

I HAD JUST THREADED MY LINE through the guides, attached a fly to my tippet, and was ready to cast when the uninvited fisherman emerged from the curtain of alders near the river's bend. In a rushed act of desperate deceit, I hooked the fly to one of the rod's guides, tightened the line around the reel and walked casually downstream, toward the man and away from My Spot. Fortunately, I hadn't begun to fish in what I—and only I—know is the best spot on the river.

"Any luck?" the man asked as we paused for our semiformal exchange.

"A typical slow evening. But, what the heck, it's great to be out, isn't it?"

"Sure is. But I wouldn't mind getting onto a good fish now and then," the man said.

"I hear ya. But that's why they call it fishing and not catching."

Satisfied that I had scored a two-to-one victory in our brief battle of streamside clichés, I wished the man luck and continued my deceptive downstream dance.

I glanced over my shoulder and watched the man pause to make a few unremarkable casts and then continue his careless wade through what was doubtless the best water he'd ever fished. Though more casts wouldn't have helped. He was standing where he should be fishing and fishing where he should be standing. I know this because I used to stand where he stood and fish where he fished. Used to, that is, before I learned the secret.

I learned—better yet, earned—the secret by virtue of a piscatorial skill that sets me apart from all my fellow fishermen: I am the best chub fisherman in the Upper Peninsula of Michigan. I don't generally target the chub like I do the brown, brook, and rainbow trout, but when one of those thick-bodied, round-mouthed fish feeds from the surface on an otherwise slow day, I will—with excessive care and undue skill—offer them my fly. Provided, of course, that no one is watching.

And so it was on a hot summer day several years ago that I cast to the barely perceptible rise of *Semotilus atromaculatus* in the exact spot where the flailing fisherman stood to cast today. And just as a creek chub is wont to do, the fish sucked my fly from the stream's surface leaving a tiny halo as the sole sign of its gluttonous assault. Responding with a leisurely snap of my wrist, I prepared to skate the stubby minnow across the river when, with great surprise and much greater delight, I saw *Salmo trutta* erupt from the river and exchange my chub and my fly for his secret.

My Spot—the place where the unknowing fisherman stood to cast—is a magical Shangri-La in an otherwise unexceptional river. Large trout love the place. A current seam funnels nearly every passing bug through a four-foot wide channel, and cool water from a spring seep moderates the temperature throughout the hot summer months. My Spot's splendor is matched only by its subtlety: its insect hatches are sparse; its current seam is nearly indiscernible;

its temperature gradient is faint and confined; and its large trout leave inconspicuous rise forms when they feed from its surface. I am the only person who knows this, and I knowingly lie, mislead, and evade to keep it that way.

I waited until the dilettante fisherman was out of sight for nearly ten minutes before cautiously returning to My Spot. My unwelcome guest was wading upstream, but, if he returned through this section just as I was onto a nice fish, my secret would be lost. Unwilling to wager with such high stakes, I decided to vacate My Spot and return the next day. The fish would still be there, but my unwanted visitor would not.

As I always do, though, I first walked downstream—just out of sight of My Spot—then entered the woods and circled back toward my car. Treachery is, after all, one of my finest fishing skills. I was on a small game trail about a hundred yards from the river when I heard a branch break near the water. I froze, hunkered, and scanned the woods for the source of the sound.

It was the man. *The Amateur. The Bumbler.* But something seemed different as he worked his way back toward My Spot. With the stealth of a coyote and the caution of a whitetail, he warily picked a winding path through the bushes and branches, and then stood beside the river and carefully scanned the water's surface, staring precisely at the place where—only 30 minutes before—he had waded carelessly and cast unremarkably.

Then a fish rose in My Spot. The man pulled several yards of line from his reel, and, void of his earlier ineptitude, he waded carefully and cast remarkably. His tiny fly drifted flawlessly downstream, then disappeared through the ring of a barely perceptible rise. He lifted his rod to set the hook, and a large trout responded with an aerial dance to the screeching song of the whirling reel. And there, on a game trail about a hundred yards away, The Greenhorn watched in doleful disbelief.

Secrets

> *Fishermen acquire the talent.*
> *They start out lying to themselves and, before they know it,*
> *they're lying to anyone who'll listen.*
>
> Paul Quinnett

THE LATIN WORD FOR WITNESS is *testis*, which—according to ancient lore—arose because male Romans testifying in court were required to place one hand over their "jewels" as they swore to tell the truth, the whole truth and nothing but the truth. Thanks to the sensible evolution of modern law, this threat has since weakened to the more reasonable *pains and penalties of perjury*, but even that is too much for most of us to tolerate, so we fishermen swear no oaths.

We lie because people expect us to. But unlike the duplicitous politician with one hand on your shoulder and the other in your pocket, we mean no harm. We revise and stretch the truth to protect our egos and reputations from the woeful certainty that most of our casts do not catch fish, and—unless we fish in Lake Woebegone—

most of the fish we catch are smaller than average. To paraphrase C. S. Lewis, pride gets no pleasure out of catching some fish, only out of catching more and bigger fish than the next guy.

Here in the Upper Peninsula of Michigan, another type of fish story protects our secret places—our Shangri-Las—from the harsh reality that the truly great places to fish are great because few people fish them. Understandably, then, the few fortunate fishermen who find these places guard their secrets with the most noble sort of fish story. "Ever fish the North Branch?" you ask. "No," they lie.

On occasion, a person who is motivated by self-pride and a compulsive need for the approval of others will stumble into great fishing. Believing that the coveted status of local fishing demigod is finally within their grasp, they draw maps, guide trips, and do whatever it takes to convince all of their friends and most of their foes that they have found and experienced spectacular fishing. John Voelker called these people *kiss-and-tell fishermen,* and, without exception, he did not fish with them. "Most fishermen swiftly learn," he wrote, "that it's a pretty good rule never to show a favorite spot to any fisherman you wouldn't trust with your wife."

When a kiss-and-tell fisherman sees great fishing destroyed by their own self-aggrandizing actions, the results are almost always chronic and severe. "'Tis better to have loved and lost than never to have loved at all" is wonderful counsel for matters as simple and common as personal relationships, but Lord Tennyson's creed rings hollow for something as complex and rare as great fishing. Experience, many have said, is something you don't get until just after you need it, and there is nothing—absolutely nothing—that a fisherman with this type of experience will do to endanger their fishing again.

Several years ago a friend who spends a few weeks each summer in the Upper Peninsula asked if I'd take him fishing. He's a good guy, I thought, and, what the heck, most of the year he lives over a thousand miles away, so I took him to one of my favorite spots. The place is remote enough to feel like it's out there, but still accessible enough that it's easy to get there. I explained the harm the wrong people could inflict on a place like this, and he seemed to understand.

This past summer I ran into my friend and a couple of his cousins who, unlike my friend, do not live over a thousand miles away. They were going fishing the next day and my friend asked if I could recommend some spots for them to try.

"Don't worry," he whispered as he pulled me aside, "I won't tell them about your secret place." He opened his gazetteer to the region they planned to fish, and I started to show them a few widely-known spots with easy access and decent fishing.

"What's that?" one of the cousins asked as he pointed his chunky finger— notable for what I recognized as worm dirt under his fingernail—toward a red circle drawn around a river bend with the frightful designation *Tim Schulz Honey Hole!!!!*

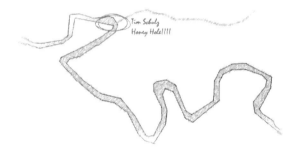

"Get over it, Tim. You don't own the river," Roxanne said while I pouted and brooded for the next several weeks. Her wisdom exceeds mine on many matters, but this is something she simply does not understand.

With assistance from the fine people of the Glenlivet distillery, I worked my way through denial, anger, bargaining and depression, and was just finishing with acceptance when I received a compelling note from my friend Jerry Dennis:

> *If I could get up your way today and tomorrow could you fish?*
> *This is wild-hair time. Need a getaway.*

Jerry's book *A Place on the Water* is one of the first books I read about fishing and living in the Upper Peninsula, and, in addition to helping me stay positive and optimistic during a difficult and challenging time in my life, his book has been a guide for the way I view the outdoors in general and the Upper Peninsula in particular. The comfort and joy I've received from Jerry's writing should have been enough, but one sentence he wrote in another book settled it:

> *Maybe, just maybe, if you strapped me to a chair with barbed*
> *wire, shoved ice picks under my fingernails, set fire to my hair,*
> *and crushed my toes one after another with pliers, I'd tell you*
> *where I caught that big brown trout last summer.*

After the catastrophe with the cousins I swore I'd never share a fishing spot again, but, geez, if I couldn't trust Jerry with a secret spot, then who could I trust? So I took him to a place that was even better than my no-longer-secret honey hole.

A few weeks after his visit, I met up with Jerry in the Lower Peninsula and he was an awful mess. His head was devoid of hair and covered in ghastly scars, his feet were mangled and confined by calf-high casts, and his fingers were so badly swollen that he could barely grasp the crutches he used to steady his stance. My immediate concern, of course, was that he had cracked and given up my spot, but his proud smile and subtle wink assured me that my secret was still safe.

Jerry was returning the favor. He took me and a few of his friends to a secret place he called Alligator Bend, and although I didn't catch many fish, I made some new friends, and one of them was a talented artist named Chad who later in the week took me to a secret place he called The River, or something like that. On my way back to the Upper Peninsula, I visited another dear friend named Adam and he took me to a secret place he called The Creek. A blissful week of fishing, and none of it would have happened if my friends hadn't shared their secrets with me.

Lewis Carroll said that one of the deep secrets of life is that all that is really worth the doing is what we do for others, and this is the challenge of the fisherman's secret spot. Voelker didn't warn us to never share our secret places; he only warned us to pick our partners well.

Fishing with a Worm

BLISS PERRY WAS A PIONEER in American literature. He taught at Williams, Princeton and Harvard, and edited the works of Ralph Waldo Emerson, among others. But I wouldn't know anything about Professor Perry if he hadn't written a book called *Fishing with a Worm*.

His short book—published in 1916—begins with an indictment of the fishing gene:

> *A defective logic is the born fisherman's portion. He is a pattern of inconsistency. He does the things which he ought not to do, and he leaves undone the things which other people think he ought to do.*

Which is, I suspect, the sort of thing that could be chiseled onto my headstone. Motivated by the simple observation that "fly-fishing has had enough sacred poets celebrating it already," Perry closes his extended parable with this:

For life is not easy, after all is said. It is a long brook to fish, and it needs a stout heart and a wise patience. All the flies there are in the book, and all the bait that can be carried in the box, are likely to be needed ere the day is over. But, like the Psalmist's "river of God," this brook is "full of water," and there is plenty of good fishing to be had in it if one is neither afraid nor ashamed of fishing sometimes with a worm.

I can't remember how or when I stumbled onto this book, but I can remember that I've read it at least once every winter since. And though it had been many years since I baited a hook with a worm, I decided one winter to do the next best thing. I tied a dozen San Juan worms.

I can't think of a fly that is easier to tie than the San Juan worm. I can tie one in about the same time it takes to impale a real worm on a hook. The only downsides to these "flies" are that they take up a lot of space in my fly box, and some fishermen—the type of folks that Perry said "always fish as if they were being photographed"—might look down their noses at me.

I wasn't sure if or when I'd fish my worms that year, but after a hard rain a few days before the trout season opener, a legion of small earthworms scattered across my driveway and I realized that my new flies might be the perfect match for this hatch.

On opening day on a remote river in the Ottawa National Forest, I tied one of my worms in tandem with a size 16 black stonefly nymph that I bought from the guy at the Laughing Loon Emporium in Iron River.

"Most people fish a big fly for this bug, but these small ones work much better," he told me. I'd tied some in that size already, but I have a simple arrangement with this man when I visit his store. He answers my "where's the best place to catch a trout in Iron County" question, and I buy a dozen of his flies.

118

Just like the guy predicted, most of the fish took the small stonefly. I'm convinced, though, that my gaudy worm attracted them to the rig, and a few fish actually took the worm.

Two days later I resolved to try my worm and stonefly tandem on a local stream. Because all of the nearby rivers were still too cold to be "on," I took the opportunity to hike into a remote location that I rarely fish after things get going. Two-and-a-half miles each way is just too much of a journey when shorter hikes are usually more productive. Once on the river, I flipped my rig into the likely spots and caught enough brook trout to keep me from thinking about the long hike out. Then, on a drift behind a substantial rock in the middle of the stream, I lifted my rod for what I believed was a light take, and—with a quick forward surge—a heavy fish promptly snapped the stonefly nymph from my line. It could have been a large brook trout, but, because this river has an unobstructed flow into Lake Superior, it might have been a steelhead. I knew there could be steelhead in this river, but I wasn't prepared for that kind of battle. Planning to catch a few native brook trout, I'd brought a 4 weight bamboo rod with 4X tippet.

People who know me well say that—at times—I have a tendency to overthink things. This was one of those times. What if that was a steelhead? There is no way I can land one of those with this rod and 4X tippet. I have some small stoneflies that are similar to the ones the guy at Laughing Loon sold me, but they aren't exactly the same, and I only have one of his left to use as a pattern. Maybe I should just walk around this hole and avoid losing that last fly.

I know about my tendency to overthink, though, so I fought off my demon, tied on the fly and continued to cast. A dozen casts later a fish bent my rod in a way that no brook trout in Michigan has ever bent a rod, nor ever will. The steelhead hurtled its body out of the river and then darted in the general direction of its summer home in

Lake Superior. Luckily, this section of the small river is uncharacteristically straight, and its narrow flow contains one downed tree, but few other line-breaking obstructions.

When I landed the fish and saw that she had taken the worm, I thought once again about a passage from Professor Perry's unique book:

> But angling's honest prose, as represented by the lowly worm, has also its exalted moments. "The last fish I caught was with a worm," says the honest Walton, and so say I.

And so say I.

Trophies

WHEN MY FRIEND Jerry Dennis invited me to join him, Chad Pastotnik, James McCullough, and Tim Tebeau for a few days on the Trophy Waters of the Au Sable River, I worried that I would be out of place in this group of tremendously talented writers and artists. But just as I've come to know Jerry to be, these guys are as kind and humble as they are talented, so I was fine. To be safe, though, I vowed to keep my mouth shut and let them think I was a fool rather than open it and remove all doubt, which, for instance, might happen if I tried to impress them with some overused quotation from Mark Twain.

As I anticipated, the guys were cerebral and witty in a writer and artist sort of way, but when Jerry told us that we were going to fish at a place called Alligator Bend where he had caught some huge fish several years ago with his friends Kelly Galloup and Bob Linseman, a little prompting by me started something akin to a demonic possession within this group of distinguished scholars.

"Hell ya, man, I wanna snag a gator."

"I can't wait to stick some of those pigs."

"Yeah baby, we're gonna snare some toads."

"Let's stop talking and go bag a donkey."

Oh my, I thought, this could be my chance to get a trophy. Finally, I would bring home a special memento to hang on my wall and show to my friends while I tell them about the night I fished Alligator Bend with the men of letters. This sort of thing is never easy, though, and many years ago—in the process of teaching me to fish—my mom showed me that the scene doesn't always follow the script when you target a trophy.

You see, my mom's relationship with fish was distinguished by a simple four-step procedure:

Catch them. Clean them. Fry them. Eat them.

With few exceptions, steps two through four always followed step one. Sure, she occasionally threw the small ones back, but she never "released" them. People born in 1921 and raised in Boskydell, Illinois didn't know any other way, I suppose.

My first lessons from the Beulah Marie Holliday school of fishing involved a cane pole, a plastic bobber and a clump of garden worms— or night crawlers when she could afford them—impaled on a bright Eagle Claw hook. Her equipment was slightly more sophisticated. Using a fiberglass rod with a Zebco 33 reel, she propelled a convoluted arrangement of swivels and hooks as close to the center of the pond as she could manage. A lead bank-sinker provided the energy for her launches, and also served to keep her line tight enough to cut cheese after she secured her rod in its spiral holder and clamped a small metal bell to the tip of the rod to signal when a fish had taken the bait. When she was satisfied that everything was as it should be, she'd return to her aluminum chair and fire up a Winston. "I'm just dying for a cigarette," she'd usually declare, which was much more true than she imagined at that time.

After I mastered the cane pole, my mom gave me a small rod with a Zebco 202 reel and a little tackle box stocked with swivels, hooks, bank sinkers, a spiral rod holder, and a small metal bell. To maximize my efficiency, she taught me the difference between the way the bell sounded when only one bluegill was hooked versus the way it sounded with two. "No need to bring in your line with only one fish," she would say. Fishing from the bank of some small Illinois farm pond, my mom and I would repeat her process until we filled our white styrofoam cooler with enough bluegills to feed the two of us and several guests. Then she'd load our gear into her Plymouth and drive us home.

That's pretty much the way I fished until a railroad conductor who patronized my mom's tavern gave me some old *Field & Stream* magazines. Poring over those pages, I learned that if you knew what you were doing—and several articles in those magazines explained exactly what you needed to know—you could catch a trophy. Fishing, I realized, could be about more than food. If everything went right, you could catch a fish big enough to mount on your wall, and all your friends would marvel in awe.

"Can I try to catch a trophy?" I asked my mom. Occasionally we would catch a small catfish during our bluegill harvests, but we hadn't really targeted them. If we did try to catch a catfish, I reasoned, we could probably get a trophy. The night before our trophy trip, my mom put two frozen packages in our sink to thaw. One was a box of shrimp she had bought at the grocery store; the other was a package of chicken livers she had gathered from chickens she had killed, plucked, and cleaned in our yard.

When we got to the pond, my mom replaced our single-barb hooks with big ugly three-pronged gaffs. Mom loaded her hooks with chicken livers; I rigged mine with shrimp. We cast, attached the bells, then began to wait. We would normally have well over a dozen bluegills in our cooler by the time my mom had smoked six cigarettes, but today she was on her seventh and the bells were still silent. My mom was about to switch to small hooks and worms when the water abruptly boiled with raindrops and we scurried back to the Plymouth, where, from my perch on the front seat, I could look over the hood and see the little golden bell on the tip of my rod. I would lose sight of my rod during the heavy sheets of rain, but between the water surges I could see it. Until the time that I couldn't.

My mom must have noticed first because she opened her door and yelled "Let's go!" I jumped out of the car, saw the rod bent nearly to the water and heard the distinctive screech of the Zebco's drag. My mom handed me the rod and said something about keeping the tip high.

The state record for a channel catfish in Illinois was in the neighborhood of 40 or 45 pounds, but my 15-pound trophy got plenty of attention in the local hardware store where we took the fish to have it weighed. When we got home my mom nailed the fish's head to a tree so she could skin it before slicing its thick flesh into chunky filets. Alas, my trophy hung on a tree for a short time, but never on a wall. She did put its severed head in our freezer, though, and for the next few months she proudly showed the frozen souvenir to everyone who visited our house.

Although I fished the Trophy Waters with my creative friends until well after dark, we snagged no gators, stuck no pigs, snared no toads, nor bagged no donkeys. But none of the guys seemed concerned about this, and we held a triumphant celebration upon our return to the cabin. Chad played music from a portable speaker system he had constructed from old tobacco cans, and we feasted on peanuts, cheese sticks, and crackers while we drank every drop of Tim's imported Scotch "one more wee dram" at a time. And of course we told stories and jokes.

Writers and artists have a way of seeing things that the rest of us can't until they show them to us, and sometime between the first Joshua Davis song and the last dram of Scotch, my friends helped me realize that we had indeed caught a trophy that night. It came to hand during a rushed moment just before we launched our expedition, and now, in a modest frame behind a plate of glass, the trophy hangs on my office wall where I proudly show it to friends while I tell them about the memorable night that I fished Alligator Bend with the men of letters.

How to Catch the Biggest Brook Trout of Your Life, Again

> *Those who cannot remember the past*
> *are condemned to repeat it.*
> George Santayana

THE FIRST TIME I caught the biggest brook trout of my life, I was so excited that I was compelled to write a how-to essay called—boldly enough—"How to Catch the Biggest Brook Trout of Your Life." Although I thought I was doing the fishing world a great service, the reactions to my accomplishment and advice were tepid:

> *That's the biggest brook trout you've ever caught? You have got to be kidding me.*

> *I tried your method, I didn't catch the biggest brook trout of my life, but my friend is pissed now because I drank two of his beers. Thanks for nothing.*

I knew I shouldn't have written it in the first place, and I swore I wouldn't repeat my mistake, but then it happened. I caught the biggest brook trout of my life, again.

Dave McMillan and his sons David and Brian invited me for a weekend at their camp, which is actually a full service cabin with electricity, running water and a septic system, but people who live in the Upper Peninsula call places like that "camps." I'm not sure why, but we do.

The camp is somewhere between Munising and Escanaba, and thanks to the "shortest route" feature on my GPS, I drove the last twenty miles on a two-track dirt road that passed by several camps that actually deserved to be called camps. Despite lacking any visible evidence that these camps housed anything that someone might want to steal, they were all protected by massive chains and signs that said "Trespassers will be shot," or something like that. Somewhere along the way I drove by a van with no windows—the sort of vehicle that some people might call a molester van—and the two bearded men beside the van appeared to be burying a body. When I finally made it to Dave's camp and said something about the van, he and the boys seemed to know who the guys were. When I told them about the body, they laughed and said that the men were likely burying a deer carcass, but, either way, it was probably a good thing that I didn't stop.

Like nearly every part of the Upper Peninsula, the land around Dave's camp is drained by a myriad of rivers, streams, and brooks, and most of those hold trout. We fished one of them with poor results the first night I arrived, so we decided to explore some different water the next evening. Brian worked during the day, and Dave needed to meet with a logger who was cutting down a bunch of beech trees on his property that either had, or would soon have, beech bark disease. That left David and me to scout for new water, and that's when

127

I caught the biggest brook trout of my life, again. And although it didn't work out so well last time, I once again believe I know something so important that I have to share it.

Just as with my first instructions, you'll need a fishing partner because you can't do this alone. I used to believe that it should be someone you hadn't fished with before, but now I believe it is important that this be someone you have fished with before. Someone like Dave McMillan, Jr. for me.

Next, pick a place that neither of you are familiar with. When you get to the river, play rock-paper-scissors, odds and evens, red hands, thumb war, or any other seemingly random way to decide which one of you will explore upstream and which one will explore downstream. You cannot make this decision in some nonrandom way. Think about it. If you could make nonrandom decisions that lead you to catch the biggest brook trout of your life, you'd probably already have done it. Right?

Once you've decided which direction each of you will go, offer to swap directions. Your friend will decline, but it is important that it doesn't look like you rigged the game in your favor, especially when you later reveal that you caught the biggest brook trout of your life.

Because you're scouting a river you've never fished before, and because you'd like to catch the biggest brook of your life (again), you should tie on a large, meaty streamer. Not too large for some of the smaller fish to chase, but large enough to move some of the big ones. A lot of different streamers would work, but I'd recommend a yellow Madonna, maybe in size 4 or 6.

You'll want to cast your fly up tight against all the downed trees and other tangles, so it will help to have several streamers in your box. You'll lose a few if you are doing this right, but be sure to have at least one streamer left when you come to a nice pool in a bend below a long, fast riffle. Cast to the front of the pool first, right where the riffle dumps its water. A nice fish will dart from the darkness and take a slash at your fly, but it's okay if you miss that one. That won't be the biggest brook trout of your life, but that fish will cause you to pay better attention, and when you cast a little deeper into the pool, tight against a large underwater log, you'll know what happened as soon as the fish takes your fly.

The next steps are optional, and, though catching the biggest brook trout of your life should be enough, they really do add to the fun. Be sure to take some photos of any smaller trout that you catch before you catch the big one. Then, of course, take several photos of the big trout. When you meet up with your friend, tell him that you caught a few fish, but nothing spectacular. Once you are in the truck and driving back to camp, hand him your camera and tell him that he can check out the fish on the display. Try not to smile when he gets to the pictures of your big fish and screams "What the hell is that? That is the biggest brook trout I've ever seen."

The Last Day

What can I say, that hasn't been said by scores?
Jimmy Buffett

A S THE SUN SANK behind the large maple at the end of our drive-way, the last day morphed into the last night and I sorted through the last photos. Another trout season had served up its magic, and I wanted to tell the story.

But what could I say about this topic that hadn't been said before? I searched the internet for "the last day of trout season" and, as I suspected, this theme had been well-flogged by fly fishing writers. Then I glanced at my bookshelf and remembered that this topic had been masterfully covered by two of my favorite writers. "The Last Day" is the last of John Voelker's essays in *Trout Madness*, and "Last Day" is the last of Jerry Dennis's essays in *The River Home*. Two magnificent writers with two splendid essays. What would I try next? Maybe a book about an old marlin fisherman, and I would begin with "He was an old man who fished alone."

No, I would not write an essay about The Last Day. But I would reread the essays by Voelker and Dennis, and I would fantasize about sitting along the shores of Frenchman's Pond or some other Place on the Water listening to these two fishermen reflect on the end of another trout season.

Perhaps we would make a few half-hearted casts. Perhaps we would take a few whole-hearted sips of bourbon. And perhaps, with a little coaxing between casts and sips, the enduring lines from their essays would flow from their lips with all the beauty and grace that flows from the pages of their books. And that would be all that needed to be said.

Tim: Where did the time go? The cold and fish-less days of late April and early May. The inconsistent but often spectacular days of late May. The glorious insect hatches of June. The dog days of July and August, when, dare I say, we sometimes target bass. The cool and colorful days of September. It all happens too fast.

John: *Each year it is the same: this time, we tell ourselves, the doze and stitch and murmur of summer can never end; this season time will surely stand still in its tracks. Yet the hazy and glorious days glide by on golden wings, and presently here and there the leaves grow tinted by subtle fairy paintbrushes and flash their red warnings of impending fall.*

Jerry: *It's like youth. You think it will never end, but it does. One day you wake up and it's October.*

Tim: It's a bittersweet time for me. I am overcome by both a sense of sadness and a feeling of fulfillment.

John: *To this fisherman, at least, with all of its sadness and nostalgia the end of fishing is not unmixed with a sense of relief and release.*

Jerry: *The last day should be taken slowly, like a last meal, so you can absorb enough sights, sounds, and scents to last through the winter. It is a day to spend sitting in a warm spot on the bank thinking of the season that is ending and the seasons yet to come.*

Tim: What about the fishing? Is the last day a day to fish, or is it all about the ritual?

Jerry: *While it lasts, that autumn fishing can be very good. The rivers are usually in good shape, the water clear, the bottom vivid with colored stones and fine, emerald algae. On the surface the water glints blue and gold and khaki, each riffle tipped with glittering bits of mirror. But you rarely see big fish feeding during bright September days. You learn to lower your expectations.*

John: *The fisherman's last-day funeral litany is a foggily beautiful and self-deceiving thing and runs something like this: the fishing is no longer sporting; the fisherman himself is dog-tired; the rise can no longer be depended on; the spawn-laden trout are far too easy to catch; and to take them now is to bite off one's nose. Amen.*

Tim: Some of our rivers are open throughout the year, but many are open only during the traditional season. Would it be good to have more rivers open throughout the year, or do you like it that we close down the season on many of the rivers and lakes?

Jerry: *I like it that way. It gives the trout a rest, permits them to spawn without being disturbed, and allows the imagination time to incubate. Like fields left fallow, those waters are better for being unfished most of the year. I think we benefit from such closure. Some things are worth waiting for, are better for having an opening and a closing and being sometimes unattainable.*

132

John: *Yes, and with a little luck perhaps diplomatic relations can even be restored with those strange but vaguely familiar ladies with whom we have been oh so absently sharing our bedrooms all summer long.*

Tim: So you think it is good to have a Last Day every year?

Jerry: *The first day and the last day of the season are more important than all of the other days put together.*

John: *Yes, on the last day we fisherman can try as we may to incant ourselves into hilarity and acceptance, but our hearts are chilled and our minds are numb. For what we fishermen really want is to go fishing, fishing, fishing, yes, fishing forever into the great far blue beyond . . .*

I don't know what else there is to say.

Made in the USA
Lexington, KY
08 July 2019